THE SEVEN WORDS

FROM THE CROSS

By

Raavi.John Sanakara Rao

M.A;B.D;M.Th; Ph.D

DEDICATED

To the Glory of the Lord Jesus who shed His blood,
died and rose again for me.

ACKNOWLEDGEMENT

Praise be to God the Father, who helped to write this little book about the seven words spoken on the cross. I thank God for giving me health, life, ideas, and the energy to write and print this book.

I am also thankful to all of my family members and dear friends who have prayed, supported and who are going to give suggestions.

PREFACE

I am happy to write a preface to Rev. Dr. Raavi John Sankara Rao's book, *Seven Words on the Cross*. John, as we address him lovingly is been one of the best faculty colleagues and fellow disciples in the glorious ministry of our Lord Jesus Christ for over four decades. His commitment to the work of the Lord, his people, and contexts is outstanding. While he is a professor of comparative religion, his focus has been to exalt Christ the crucified (1 Cor 1:23).

In obedience to his specific call, John and his late wife Mary, have moved out from familiar Hyderabad (South India) into God-zone Indore (North India) as a missionary couple. He remained calm when his dear wife Mary passed away due to a cardiac arrest on 17 May 2021. Mary's death happens during the harsh Covid pandemic. But his unwavering missionary commitment made him withstand bereavement in spite of compelling challenges to turn back to South India to satisfy the kith and kin. The north India challenges in ministry include strange cultural values, miss people of his mother tongue, harsh weathers and unploughed terrains for Christ. But praising his master he touches many lives of both missionaries and believers. As a result, a number of churches are established both in the North India and Nepal.

As such John's current work applies missionary principles of what it means to be a pioneer. This volume would become a dear piece of literature for both the mainline and the independent churches, especially useful during the passion week and the Good Friday seasons.

The book contains five parts: firstly, each word of Jesus spoken on the cross is related to the experiences of Old Testament saints.

Secondly, it enlivens the New Testament crucifixion scenarios.

Thirdly, it brings home what would it mean for you and me today.

Fourthly, it brings in the power of reflection to edify the believers drawing them closer to the Christ crucified and risen.

Finally, it makes bible study or house church groups to discuss the principles from multiple perspectives or contexts.

I bless the current work, recommend to you, and pray that the Lord may enable John to produce many more innovative writings to benefit the church at large and our dear nation.

Rev. Dr. E.D. Solomon. PhD.

Professor and Head Dept of Missiology

Caleb Institute, Farrukhnagar,

Gurgaon- NCR Delhi.

Haryana State. PIN-122506

Email: etaladavid1954@gmail.com

Ph: 91+ 829 6759 755, 832 859 6739

TABLE OF CONTENTS

Grandfather, are there only seven words in this entire book?", my 11-years-old grandson asked with his eyes wide open when he saw the title of the book. My child, these are not seven words, God had incarnated and had given seven great messages from the cross to the entire world.

I am very thankful that by the amazing Grace of God, my resolve to write about the seven words of Jesus on the cross, for almost five years, has been fulfilled on Good Friday 2024.

The Triune God - the Father, the Son, and the Holy Spirit, has manifested himself in different ways at different times. "In the past God spoke to our ancestors through the prophets, at many occasions and in various ways, but in these last days he has spoken to us by his Son, whom he has appointed heir of all things, and through whom he has made the universe". (Hebrews 1:1-2)

It was around 700 B.C. the prophet Isaiah prophesied that Jesus would be born conceived in a virgin womb. Prophet Micah had said around 500 AD, that He will be born in Bethlehem of Judah. It was prophesied in Genesis 3:15 that Lord Jesus would be born of a woman and crush the head of the serpent for the salvation of mankind.

The sufferings on the cross were prophesied by many, including the prophets Isaiah and Zechariah. He also clearly explained the purpose of his coming to his disciples in advance. But they didn't like it. He rebuked them and told them that this was Satan's idea. "I am the good shepherd, and the good shepherd lays down his life for the sheep". The law had repeatedly said that there is no atonement for sin without the shedding of blood. That is how he explained his cause, his reason to lay down his life. The Son of Man did not come to be ministered but to minister and to give his life as a ransom for many. He died, was buried and rose again. This is a historical fact.

The thoughts, words and deeds of the Lord Jesus on the cross revealed God's nature and His will.

It is Lord Jesus, who answered the eternal prayers of *Asatoma Sadgamaya... Tamasoma Jyotirgamaya... Mrityorma Amritangamaya.* He declared and revealed, "I am the way, I am the truth, I am the life, I am the light, I am the resurrection". (John 14.6)

According to the Gospel of John it was the day of preparation for the Passover; Jesus was executed on the day before the Passover. A sacrifice was hung on the cross. The disciple John wrote, "When they came to Jesus and saw that he was already dead, they did not break his legs (John 19.33). He died at the same time when the passover lambs were slaughtered in the temple that is about the third hour. Jesus Christ became the passover lamb, as the apostle Paul says, "Christ was sacrificed for us as the passover lamb." The innocent lamb was slayed for our sins so that we could be forgiven. This is the mission that the Lord Jesus has now fulfilled. (John 19:14, 31-34; Exodus 12:46; 1 Corinthians 5:7)

It was twelve o'clock the day when Jesus was crucified. A sign was written against him, as 'Jesus, the King of the Jews'. Darkness fell over the whole country from noon till three o'clock. The sun disappeared and the veil of the sanctum was torn in two halves. Then Jesus cried out with a loud voice and said, "Father, into your hands I commit my spirit." He said this and died. (Mark 15:25-26, Luke 23:44-46).

Every human's last words are precious and priceless. The question that is usually asked when someone dies is - what was the last thing he or she said? If the last words of a man's life are so precious, valuable and important, then are not the words spoken by the almighty God precious over all, when He came to this world and sacrificed His life for the salvation of all humankind and died on the cross?

There is no doubt that his words on the cross are important. The last words of the Lord are well described in the Holy Scripture by the four evangelists- Matthew, Mark, Luke and John.

What is the purpose of human (our) life? What does God expect?

When Abram was ninety-nine years old, Jehovah appeared to him and said, "I am the Almighty God, walk in my presence and be blameless." (Gen 17:2) This is God's purpose in our (human) life. Realizing this, Job corrected his life. Job lived in the land of Uz. This man was blameless and upright; he feared God and shunned evil. How was Job able to live a blameless and upright life? He lived his life not only with fear and responsibility that one day he would be accountable to God, he also enjoyed the presence of God every day, every hour, every minute and every second of his life. That is why he could boldly say that he would tell God the number of his steps and that he would go to God like a king. (Gen 17:1, Job 1:1, 31:37)

In his gospel, the disciple John explained the relationship between the Lord Jesus and the Heavenly Father very well. "In the beginning was the Word, the Word was with God, and the Word was God. He was with God in the beginning. The Word became flesh and dwelt among us full of grace. May we find His glory as the glory of the only begotten Son of the Father" (John 1:1,14).

Firstly, the Lord Jesus said, "I and the Father are united." (John 10:30)

I am not in the world, but they are in the world, I am coming to you. Holy Father, save them in your name, which you have blessed me with, that they may be united as we are united. (John 17:11)

Secondly, to the disciple who asked him to show the Father, Jesus answered: "Don't you know me, Philip, even after I have been among you such a long time"? Anyone who has seen me has seen the Father. How can you say, 'Show us the Father?' Don't you believe that I am in the Father, and that the Father is in me? The words I say to you I do not speak on my own authority. Rather, it is the Father, living in me, who is doing his work. Believe me when I say that I am in the Father and the Father is in me; or at least believe the evidence of the works themselves". (John 14:9-11)

Thirdly, Lord Jesus knew very well where he came from

and that He was going back to. He came from the Father into the world. And he said to them that he was leaving the world and going to the Father. (John 14:28).

Lord Jesus fulfilled the will of the Father, spoke the words of the Father and did the works of the Father. The first Adam was unable to fulfill God's will. But Jesus, the last Adam, came to fulfill the Father's will. He dedicated himself. He was a divine man. He came down to this world to reveal the invisible God.

Because of these three reasons the Lord Jesus fulfilled WWW- Will, Words, Works of the Father.

1. The Will of the Father – Jesus said, "My food is to do the will of Him who sent me and to finish His work". (John 4:34, 5:30)

2. The Words of the Father - Jesus spoke the words of the Father because he did not speak on his own but the Father who sent him gave him a commandment about what he should say and what he should speak (John 12:49). He said to them, "I am teaching what I have seen from my father, so you are doing what you have heard from your father." (John 8:28)

3. The Works of the Father - Lord Jesus did the works of the Father. He said that He who sent me is with me and He has not left me alone because I am always doing the work that He loves. Jesus gave them this answer: "Very truly I tell you, the Son can do nothing by himself; he can do only what he sees his Father doing, because whatever the Father does the Son also does.

Verily I say unto you, The Father loves the Son, and commits all things unto him. The works I do in my Father's name testify about me (John 8:29, 5:19,20, 10:25). Don't you believe that I am in the Father, and that the Father is in me? The words I say to you I do not speak on my own authority. Rather, it is the Father, living in me, who is doing his work (John 14:10). In the same way - the Father dwells in Me and speaks His words. He is doing according to his own idea.

The first Adam gave himself up to death for his wife. He is the forerunner of Lord Jesus who is the last Adam. As the last Adam, the Lord Jesus "became the Saviour" for His bride, His church. He gave himself up for his people, for this world and for his community with absolute and eternal love. He fulfilled his responsibility through God's will, words and works. He has completed this for the salvation of the entire mankind.

Among them, I desire to meditate on these words in this

little book. I am grateful to the Almighty, Omniscient, Omnipresent God for the help. The seven words spoken by Jesus on the cross were not just words. These are seven amazing messages.

In each word (message of the cross) there are five main parts besides the word spoken by the Lord.

1. Old Testament Prophecy.

2. Fulfilment in the New Testament.

3. Message

4. Application

5. Questions to be discussed.

All the readers should understand, embrace, experience and enjoy this great truth. To be heirs of God's love and eternal kingdom, they should grow daily in the company of the Father, the Son and the Holy Spirit. It is God's will and even my prayer to live a life that glorifies God and witnesses to the whole world.

THE FIRST WORD

1. Jesus said, "Father, forgive them; for they do not know what they are doing." (Luke 23:34)

1.1 Old Testament Prophecy

The Lord Jesus was fulfilling the Old Testament prophecy written about Himself by praying - Father, forgive them; for they do not know what they are doing. "And so I will give him a place of honour, a place among great and powerful men. He willingly gave his life and shared the fate of evil men" (Isaiah 53:12). From the cross the Lord Jesus pleaded for the forgiveness of sinners. He is the mediator between sinful mankind and a holy God.

As Isaiah prophesied, I will partake of him with the great ones. He divided the booty with the nobles. "He took the place of many sinners and prayed that they might be forgiven" (Isaiah 53:12).

This was fulfilled at the death of Jesus Christ. He interceded for those who persecuted and tortured him. (Luke 23:34).

1.2 Fulfillment in the New Testament

"For there is one God and one mediator between God and mankind, the man Christ Jesus, who gave himself as a ransom for all people". This has now been witnessed to at proper time.(1 Timothy 2:5-6) Through this prayer he implemented the Sermon on the Mount. "You have heard that it was said, 'Love your neighbour and hate your enemy.' But I tell you, love your enemies and pray for those who persecute you, that you may be children of your Father in heaven. Pray for those who persecute you" (Matthew 5:43-44).

The Lord Jesus prayed for his persecutors when he was being persecuted.

In addition to the forgiveness of the Lord Jesus, a fact to be noted is that those who persecuted Him did not really know what they were doing. Common people or sinners did not know why they were crucifying Jesus. They were deceived by the leaders and the high priests. Innocent people were motivated against him (Luke 23:34). It's written, I know, brothers, that through ignorance you did it, as did also your rulers. (Acts 3:17)

This is Peter's consolation:

The soldiers were Romans. They were doing their duty as per the order given to them. They might not have had any grudge against Jesus personally. They were carrying out the punishment imposed by the law. But they did not know that they were crucifying the Son of God and the Savior of the world (1 Corinthians 2:8).

This is the first word that Jesus spoke from the cross. He begged his father to forgive his enemies. It is a symbol and a clear proof of love. Jesus' words and deeds were always corresponding. He said in Matthew 5:43-44, "You have heard that it was said, 'Love your neighbour and hate your enemy'. But I tell you, love your enemies and pray for those who persecute you". He walked his talk and proved it. The Lord Jesus demonstrated His love for those who were crucifying Him.

"Father, forgive them, for they do not know what they are doing."

These words are often called the "speech of forgiveness". Jesus not only prayed for the forgiveness of the soldiers who crucified him, for the religious leaders who handed him over, but also for all mankind. And He himself asked for the forgiveness of all those who caused the death penalty. Through the crucifixion of the Lord Jesus, he gave the whole world another good chance. This is a golden opportunity to seek Him and seek His forgiveness.

Blessed is the one whose transgressions are forgiven, whose sins are covered. Blessed is the one whose sin the LORD does not count against him and in whose spirit is no deceit" (Psalms 32:1- 2).

"Blessed are those, who understand the truth, accept God and walk in His footsteps both individually and collectively. Blessed is the nation whose God is the LORD, the people he chose for his inheritance" (Psalms 33:12).

Why did Jesus pray this prayer?

Jesus prayed this prayer because forgiveness is God's nature. Nehemiah proclaimed this fact in his fasting prayer. God's nature is to forgive His children. But human nature is to 'rebel'. Nehemiah 9:17 clearly illustrates these two points.

"They were unwilling to obey, but they did not remember the miracles you have done among them. They hardened their minds and rebelled against you, asking for a leader to return them to the land of slavery from which they came. But you are the God ready to forgive, merciful, long-suffering and merciful, and did not forsake them".

The first word spoken by the Lord Jesus on the cross was - They don't know what they are doing. But the Lord Jesus knew everything. There is nothing that is not known to him. That is, Jesus knew not only the deeds, but also the words and thoughts of the Jewish high priests, scribes, authorities, soldiers, etc. (Luke 6:8). A man is a combination of these three - thoughts, words and deeds. The triple purification of these three areas is not seen in the human society. All three are corrupted because of sinful nature and influence. Jesus prayed for the forgiveness of all sins.

The prodigal son and the second thief on the cross came to their senses and asked the Lord Jesus for forgiveness. Both of them benefited (Luke 15:17, 23:42-43).

Receiving forgiveness or healing, which is important?

Lord Jesus Himself showed what is important to humanity. Receiving Forgiveness or healing? Which is more important, the salvation of the soul or the health of the body? Both are needed, but which comes first? The Lord Jesus explained this. By healing a paralytic on a sabbath day, he declared that the atonement of sin was more important than the healing of the body. "But you must know that the Son of

Man has authority on earth to forgive sins," he told the scribes.

"He said to the paralytic, I say to you - Arise, take up your bed, and go home." Because of this saying, we know that his sins were forgiven. (Mark 2:8-12) By saying this, healing the paralytic, Jesus proved that forgiveness of sins is in the first place, even though healing is needed; he proved, it was secondary.

The Process and Procedure of Forgiveness:

How is a woman caught in adultery forgiven?

Lord Jesus went to the Mount of Olives. When he returned to the temple in the morning, all the people came to him. Jesus sat down and taught them. The Scribes and the Pharisees brought a woman caught in adultery. Made her to stand in the middle, "Teacher, this woman was caught in the act of adultery. Moses commanded us in the law to stone them to death (In Leviticus 20:10 it's written to kill both of them) but what do you say?

When they were asking him repeatedly, he was scribbling on the ground, he looked up and said, "Whoever is without sin among you should be the first to throw a stone at her." He bent down again and wrote on the ground. (Perhaps He was writing their sins!) According to Jeremiah 17:1 Judah's sins are written with the tip of a diamond - i.e. no one can erase).

But after hearing him say so, they went out one by one, starting from the oldest to the youngest. Finally, only Jesus was left. The woman stood in the middle. Jesus looked up and said, "Woman, where are they? Has no one condemned you"? She said, no one sir. "Then neither do I condemn you," Jesus declared. "Go now and leave your life of sin."(John 8:1-11)

How did Lord Jesus forgive this sinner?

Among the many purposes of Jesus' coming, two of the most important ones are mentioned here - namely, to fulfil the law (Matthew 5:17) and to seek and save the sinners (Luke 19:10).

1. Do not think that I have come to abolish the Law or the Prophets; I have not come to abolish them but to fulfil them, said the Lord. (Matthew 5:17) The law means truth, justice, which means that the sinner must be punished.

2. The second purpose, he said, was to seek and save the lost. That is, He came to forgive the sinner. The Lord Jesus made this clear when he came to Zacchaeus' house. He told Zacchaeus that the Son of Man had come to seek and save what was lost. (Luke 19:10)

These two words - fulfilling the law and saving the sinner are contradictory. Matthew 5:17, Luke 19:10.

Truth or Grace

Punish the sinner or Forgive the sinner?

Generally speaking, it is never meeting like East and West; like two train tracks that never meet. But do you know what did the Lord Jesus say and what did He do?

"For truly I tell you, until heaven and earth disappear, not the smallest letter, not the least stroke of a pen, will by any means disappear from the Law until everything is accomplished". (Matthew 5:18) That is, both of these must be fulfilled.

How did the Lord Jesus fulfil everything?

In the beginning was the Word, the Word was with God, and the Word was God. As the Word became flesh and dwelt among us full of grace. We shall see his glory as the glory of the only begotten Son of the Father (John 1:1, 14).

In one such example, the frog dies if the snake is told to satisfy its hunger. If you tell the snake not to eat, the snake will die of hunger. If a snake is fed, a frog should loose it's life. How!!!

Likewise, with truth and grace; if you succeed in one, you fail in the other. The words of the Lord Jesus never fail. Heaven and earth may pass away, but my words will never pass away, said the Lord Jesus. He is the replica of grace and truth.

Who is this Lord Jesus? This Jesus is one hundred percent full of grace and one hundred percent full of truth. Not even one percent less in any one of these two.

We have six subjects in class 10. One hundred marks for each subject means total 600 marks should be obtained. If God writes 10th class exams, He must get 600 marks compulsorily. If He gets even 599 He is not at all God.

Similarly another name of God is - *Sakala Sadguna Sampoornudu. Sakala* means all, All means 100 percent. *Sadguna (Virtue)* means good qualities. Absolute means hundred percentage perfect. Lord Jesus is rich in virtues. He is omniscient, omnipotent and omnipresent. All of him is perfect. Jesus is full of grace and truth.

What we need to realize is that, the Lord Jesus does not look at people but he looks at the problem first, then people and solves their problems.

In this event, if we look at the "person" first (John 8), speaking to the adulterous woman, saying to her, "Woman, don't you have any sense, is there no time and context, why did you leave your husband and do this sinful thing?" If He was dealing with Scribes and the Pharisees, He would have asked, "Where is that boy? First bring him, then I will answer you." Or "Why only this girl was caught? How can adultery be done with one person? Can you clap with one hand? You need two hands to clap. So where is that boy?" But Jesus did not harass like that. He saw the problem first, and then the man.

The Lord Jesus loves the sinner but hates the sin. For this reason, He stood up and said to them, "Let any one of you who is without sin be the first to throw a stone at her". (John 8:7)

May be they all brought stones too. If He had advised according to the law, they may have beaten her or if He had said something wrong, they may have beaten Jesus. Because they were waiting for an opportune time to kill the Lord Jesus; this was their intention. His enemies were both at home (John 7:25) and outside (John 5:15, 18, 7:1).

Those who were without sin were told to throw stones at her first. All of them were shocked as if the stones they had brought fell on themselves. Everyone realized that they are sinners. They left the place starting with the elders to the children.

What did the Lord Jesus do?

Jesus is sinless and holy. So he could stone the woman to death. But that's not what he came for. Moreover, Jesus challenged the religious leaders, "Who among you can prove me a sinner? There was no one who could respond.

Yes, He is a holy God. He can punish her. But if he punishes her according to the law, his mercy would not be revealed. On the other hand, if she were to be forgiven and sent away, it would be as if the Lord Jesus had dismissed the law.

The problem is that if Jesus fulfilled the law (Matthew 5:17), He would have rejected grace. Hence, making Luke 19:10 a failure. Similarly, showing only grace (Luke 19:10) is like rejecting the law (Matthew 5:17). He would not fail His word. But what is the solution to this problem?

To fulfil truth and justice, the sinner must be punished.

To show grace and mercy, the sinner must be forgiven and saved.

How did the Lord Jesus do it?

To accomplish His work and reconcile grace and truth He said to her, "Woman, where are they? Has no one punished you?" "No, Lord," she answered. "Neither will I punish you; go and sin no more." Jesus said to her and sent her away.

Jesus got up and walked a few steps forward, where she stood; He stood in her footprints. Since she was caught red handed in sin, she may have sweated all over her face in shy and shame. As a result, her footprints may still be visible even after she left from her position. Jesus went and stood in her footprints. By this action, he took upon himself the punishment for her sins from her childhood till that time. By this action, He fulfilled (Matthew 5:17) the justice of the law and also fulfilled grace (Luke 19:10) to save the sinner.

He saved her from the death penalty. Lord Jesus is merciful. He is gracious. He is righteous. So, he fulfilled grace and executed justice.

Jesus is righteous. The sinner must be punished according to justice. But Jesus the judge, bore the punishment himself. He paid the penalty himself. He fulfilled justice by taking upon Himself her shame, her sin, her curse, and her punishment. He obeyed the truth through His interpretation. And He also showed grace. In this way Jesus fulfilled His Name as the fulfillment of grace and truth. God's love for the unworthy is called Grace. Not for the worthy. He saved her with this grace. Grace and truth - these two words, even though contradictory, He kept these two in balance.

Where did the Merciful God's grace and truth meet? Where was the fulfillment of the law and the punishment in place of the sinner fulfilled? Matthew 5:17 and Luke 19:10 Where do truth and grace meet? Where did righteousness and peace kiss each other? The answer is on the cross.

Love and truth have met together; righteousness and peace have kissed! (Psalms 85:10). Where do these conflicting truth and grace meet? On the cross of Calvary. This is the holy confluence. The shrine that sanctifies the sinner is the cross. Lord Jesus is the only bearer of the cross in this world. In our Indian culture, the place where two or three rivers meet is called a confluence. It is considered a holy place. People go and take holy bath to wash away their sins. But the true confluence is the union of grace and truth. It happened on the cross.

That is why Jesus prayed from the cross, 'Father, forgive them for they do not know what they are doing.' This prayer was accepted by God the Father. The reason is that Jesus fulfilled one hundred percent justice and one hundred percent grace. Praise be to God!

Even today, the gracious Lord Jesus is ready to forgive those who realize that they are sinners and seek forgiveness; so that those who are forgiven now may have peace, joy and happiness in this world and enjoy a life of abundance. They will have eternal life with God in the future. This is God's promise. This is the meaning and purpose of human life.

Jesus' teachings about the need for forgiveness

The Lord Jesus continued to teach forgiveness until the last moment of his life. When His disciples asked, Lord teach us to pray, he taught them to forgive our debts as we forgive our debtors (Matthew 6:12). He declared that forgiveness of sins is more important than physical healing and he repeatedly said that he has the power to forgive sins on earth (Mark 2:9, 10).

"And when you stand praying, if you hold anything against anyone, forgive them"(Mark 11:25). Not only this, "If you are offering your gift at the altar and remember that your brother or sister has something against you, leave your gift there in front of the altar. Go and be reconciled to them at first and then come and offer your gift" (Matthew 5:23,24). When we forgive each other's sins, there is peace. At the time of the Lord's Supper, He said, "My blood is for the forgiveness of sins". This is my blood of the covenant, which is poured out for many for the forgiveness of their sins (Matthew 26:28). Jesus reminded the same thing after His death and resurrection.

Again Jesus said, "Peace be with you! As the Father has sent me, I am sending you." And with that He breathed on them and said, "Receive the Holy Spirit. If you forgive anyone's sins, their sins are forgiven; if you do not forgive them, they are not forgiven."(John 20:21-23).

Jesus' advice about forgiveness of sins:

Once Peter came to Jesus and said, "Lord, how many times may my brother sin against me and I forgive him, up to seven times?" Jesus said to him, "I tell you, not seven times but seventy times seven! (Matthew 18.21-22) it means that a Christian must have the nature of forgiveness always.

John the Baptist's father, Zechariah, declared in his prophecy that God, in His great mercy, had given us the forgiveness of sins.

Zechariah was filled with the Holy Spirit and spoke God's message: "Praise be to the Lord, the God of Israel, because he has come to his people and redeemed them. He has raised up a horn of salvation for us in the house of his servant David (as he said through his holy prophets long ago), salvation from our enemies and from the hand of all who hate us— to show mercy to our ancestors and to remember his holy covenant, the oath he swore to our father Abraham: to rescue us from the hand of our enemies, and to enable us to serve him without fear in holiness and righteousness before him in all our days. And you, my child, will be called a prophet of the Most High; for you will go on before the Lord to prepare the way for him, to give his people the knowledge of salvation through the forgiveness of their sins, because of the tender mercy of our God, by which the dayspring will come to us from heaven (Luke 1:67-78).

In his ministry, Jesus forgave a paralytic (Matthew 18:21-22) and a woman caught in sin (John 8:1-11). In the Pharisee's house, Jesus forgave a woman who washed His feet with tears and wiped His feet with her hair (Luke 7:36-48).

1.3 Message

In the first of the seven words spoken on the cross - Jesus prayed, "Father, forgive them because they do not know what they are doing". Where grace and truth meet together, forgiveness of sin takes place (Psalms 85:10). Without the shedding of blood there is no forgiveness (Hebrews 9:22).

God's love should experience and demonstrate God's forgiveness. We have to prove this to others in our words and actions. Paul wrote to the Ephesian churches, "Be kind and compassionate to one another, forgiving each other, just as in Christ for God's sake has forgiven you" (Ephesians 4:32).

Jesus told a parable in which one person did the opposite way. The king lent 10,000 talents to one. (A talent is Rs 3,600 which means 3,60,00,000 or three crore sixty lakhs). From this he lent 100 dinars or Rs.50 to his friend. When the king asked him to settle his debt, the person who borrowed money, requested the lender to give him a little more time to pay. However, the king mercifully forgave him all his debt. He went back happily and asked the person who owed him 50 rupees to settle his debt. This man also asked for some time. But he forcefully arrested him and put him in prison. How unfair! That 50 rupees were not his. He gave from the three crore sixty lakh given him by the owner. If the king could forgive his debt of crores of rupees, how could he not cancel 50 rupees? Cancellation means to forgive (Matthew 18:23- 34). Isn't this a great crime?

Forgive others as God has forgiven you. This is the truth. This is right. This should be the code of relations between husband and wife in the family and among friends. In the church too, this should be the code between the pastor and the believers.

David was forgiven for his grave sins. Finally, he was praised by God as a man after His own heart. (Acts 13:22)

Jesus said during His lifetime on earth, that He had the power to forgive sins. Jesus commanded us to forgive both our friends and our enemies. He is a great role model for the whole world. He walked His talk. He didn't think about himself even though he was experiencing terrible torture, humiliation and pain. "They did not know what they are doing, so Father, forgive them" He said.

This is God's divine unconditional love. Because His Name is Love. Day or night, sadness or pleasure, shame or honour, wealthy or poor, His name is the same. It doesn't change. Similarly, God's Name is Love. God's Name is Justice. But there is an appropriate time for that. While suffering so much on the cross, if He cursed, blamed or punished them, his name would be changed. He is an unchanging God. A God who loves with unchanging love. That's the reason. He prayed this prayer with love. Why? If their sins are not forgiven, their sins will lead them to eternal hell. To protect them from eternal hell, Jesus uttered this first word for them and us while he himself suffered the punishment. Father, they do not know what they are doing, please forgive them.

The motives of Jesus asking for forgiveness of their sins:

1. They must know God's love.

2. They should seek, understand and receive the true God.

3. They must realize true self and understand that they are sinners.

4. They should seek forgiveness of sins from God.

5. They should experience God's love, peace and joy.

6. They should give thanks to God.

7. They should actively witness to others of their forgiveness of sins in love.

God said about David, "I am well pleased in him. He is a man after my own heart. He is without hypocrisy." We also need to have a good testimony from God of our righteousness. That's why this prayer - Father, forgive them for they do not know what they are doing.

1.4 Application

Read how God helped me to experience the grace of God mentioned above. I am Sankara Rao. We are five siblings. Our parents are Pushpavati and Sri Ramulu.

As per the tradition of my father, I have been involved in idolatry since childhood. Not knowing what is right and what is wrong. I was living a sinful life. In 1979, two of my friends died on the spot in a road accident. At that time I questioned myself, "where would I go if I died in the same manner?" No one knows when, where and how death would come to each of us. But death is certain. This fear gripped me. In my Hindu tradition, what I have observed is that, if you do good deeds, you will go to heaven. But if you do bad things, you will go to hell. At that moment, I knew I couldn't go to heaven because I didn't do the right things. I realized that evil deeds effect and result is hell.

Then I began to perform my ritual of worship with great devotion to escape from the torments of hell. But the same question kept bothering me, "where do you go when you die?" One of my friends told me to believe in Jesus Christ. He will answer your question. In those days, my understanding of Jesus Christ was that He is a foreign God. And He is the God of the lower castes only. But anyhow I decided to give a chance to Jesus just this time. Because even though I did not know their names, I was still worshiping 33 crore of deities.

That same week I had a dream. In that dream, I was walking with my friend. After a few minutes, I looked back. I noticed that someone is coming to kill me with a gun. I told my friend who was walking with me, "Let's run away and escape" and we started running. As we were running together, the person who was coming to kill me came faster than us and stood before me to shoot. At that moment, to save me, my friend stood between us and grabbed the gun from him. In this struggle, the bayonet of the gun (like a sword) was stuck in my friend's palm. I woke up when I saw blood.

It was a dream. But that influence worked very deep in my life. It led me to know about the Creator of the universe.

When I woke up, I had two questions. Firstly, who was that person who came to kill me? And secondly, who was the one who was wounded for me to save me?

The answer to the first question is that, the person who came to kill me is no other than my sin. Usually, we commit sin and forget, but sin does not forget us. This is a fact. And I admit it, yes, I have sinned and I am a sinner.

The second question is, who is this man who was wounded for me? "He is your Creator", my conscience told me. At that time, there were so many idols in my home, I said are these idols whom I worship are my creators. "No", came the answer. I asked, "why not?". The answer came, "They are married. They have children and grandchildren!! And God does not have or participate in sexual desire. God does not and should not have "lust", 'anger', 'greed', 'infatuation', 'pride', 'jealousy'. These are the six enemies that are oppressing the human beings. But isn't God transcendental of all these?

I began to search for the God with wounded hands. I realized that there is no one but Jesus Christ. During this searching, I said a little prayer, "God forgive me, I am a sinner." As soon as I said that to God, a great weight was lifted away from my heart. Peace and joy entered my heart.

With this joy I took the Bible and started reading. I read the Bible from the beginning to end (Genesis to Revelation). But in my first reading, I could understand nothing except one sentence from the Bible. According to 2 Samuel 18:33, Absalom was the most cruel, wicked man. He was no other than the son of King David. He conspired for the throne.

Knowing this, King David left the throne and fled into the wilderness. But Absalom, who had done many wretched deeds, went out with his army to kill his father, as if conspiring alone was not enough. Absalom died in a fierce battle. His father David, when he knew of it, wept.

The king was very upset and went up to the room and wept, wandering around, crying, "My son, Absalom, my son, Absalom, my son, how good it would be if I died instead of you, my son, Absalom, my son."

This incident reminded me of my childhood. I had lost my father when I was four years old. I don't remember much about my father. But when I was 10, my father's younger brother, one of my uncles, also died. At that time, my grandmother was crying and said, "Oh God, you are taking my sons, take me instead of them." When I read this passage, I remembered my grandmother's cry.

So, these three things come together and revealed one truth. It expresses a father's love. As I saw in the dream, my friend was wounded for me, I remembered the Bible verse which I read, David the father wanted to die for his son. The father felt that, although the son is very cruel, he should live forever and he himself should die. And in my real life, my grandmother wanted to die instead of her two sons. She cried in the same way.

And these three experiences were fulfilled in Jesus Christ. God, the creator of the universe, loved me and bore my punishment. He forgave me. He died for me. He conquered death and rose again because He is God. He conquered the death and is living.

He gave me peace, joy and eternal life. He led me from darkness to light. He led me from untruth to truth. He led me from death to immortality.

My question was answered! Where would I go when I die? This was my question. Jesus bore the penalty of my sin and death. Therefore, there is no more death for me. I will be with God forever. Even if I praise the Lord lifelong from the bottom of my heart for this assurance, it is not enough. This is the forgiveness and peace of Jesus Christ that I have experienced and continue to experience in my life. Since then, I have been following Jesus Christ as my Lord and Saviour and the reason behind this is the first word of the Lord Jesus from the cross- "Father, forgive them for they do not know what they are doing." I am blessed, what about you!

1.5 Questions to be discussed

1. Share the experience of your sins being forgiven?

2. Matthew 5:43-44 read and write down what the Lord is speaking to you.

3. Write the list of people you need to forgive.

4. After making a list, first forgive them in your heart, then
    go and make peace with them.

2. TODAY YOU WILL BE WITH ME IN PARADISE" (LUKE 23:43)

Jesus answered him, "Truly I tell you, today you will be with me in paradise" (Luke 23:43).

Jesus spoke these words to a criminal on the cross – this Word reveals God's special love for those who turn to Him in faith. This second word is called the "salvation Word".

According to the Gospel of Luke, Jesus was crucified along with two thieves. One of them was surprised to see the blamelessness, love and spirit of forgiveness of the Lord Jesus. Despite being sinless and even after bearing so much of suffering, He does not say anything to those who persecute Him. Moreover, He prays for the forgiveness of the evil-doers because He knows that they do not know what they are doing. The thief believed that He is not a common man, He is God Himself in human form and He is the Saviour of sinners. So, he prayed to Jesus to remember him when He comes again into His kingdom.

2.1 Old Testament Prophecy

As the prophet Isaiah said, "Because he poured out his life unto death, and was numbered with the transgressors. For He bore the sin of many, and made intercession for the transgressors" (Isaiah 53:12). Trespass means one who goes out of order, one who defies authority and one who rebels. But Jesus has no relation with anything of this nature, not even a small part in it. These titles of trespasser and transgressor do not belong to Him. Moreover, He challenged, "Can any of you prove me guilty of sin?"(John 8:46). There was no one, who could respond to His challenge. The reason is that the Lord Jesus is perfect in all virtues. His Name is Holy and Perfect (John 1:14, Psalms 99:3,5,9).

Prophecy about Judas Iscariot - There are two prophecies given by prophets Zechariah and David. The first speaks of the price or profit of being unfaithful. The next one is about the condition of the betrayed person.

I told them, "If you think it to be best, give me my pay; if not, keep it with yourself." So, they paid me thirty pieces of silver. And the LORD said to me, "Throw it to the potter"— the handsome price at which they valued me! So, I took the thirty pieces of silver and threw them at the potter in the house of the LORD. (Zechariah 11:12,13)

In those days Peter stood up among the believers (a group numbering about a hundred and twenty) and said, "Brothers and sisters, the Scripture had to be fulfilled in which the Holy Spirit spoke long ago through David concerning Judas, who served as guide for those who arrested Jesus. He was one of us and shared in our ministry." (With the payment he received for his wickedness, Judas bought a field; there he fell headlong, his body burst open and all his intestines spilled out. Everyone in Jerusalem heard about this, so they called that field in their language Akeldama, that is, Field of Blood.) "For," said Peter, "it is written in the book of Psalms: "'May his place be deserted; let there be no one to dwell in it,' and, "'May another take his place of leadership' (Psalms 69:25, Acts 1:15-20).

While Jesus was hanging on the cross, Judas Iscariot, the traitor, convinced in his soul that he had betrayed the 'innocent', went back to the religious leaders to return the money. They refused to take it back. But Judas threw the money into the temple and left. (Matthew 27:5) He threw the silver in the holy place and left. After that he went and committed suicide by hanging himself. He fell headlong, his body burst open and all his intestines spilled out. He died. But who buried his body?

Finally, one of the criminals on the cross realized that he

deserved the punishment for his sin. No one enjoys the money earned by cheating and betrayal for a long period of time. This is a proven truth. Anyone who is hung on a pole is under God's curse (Deuteronomy 21:23). This prophecy is fulfilled in Luke 23:43.

Jesus lived a righteous and holy life in exchange for their reproaches. Moreover, he obeyed the authorities. He also paid tax. He did not rebel. He did not transgress in thoughts, words or actions.

Yet, Jesus was crucified among evildoers and criminals. Hence the challenge of counting him as a transgressor appears. Nevertheless, all the prophecies foretold concerning his life and death were fulfilled, including the one of being counted among transgressors.

2.2 Fulfillment in the New Testament

According to Luke 23:32-38, two other men, both criminals, were also led out with Jesus to be executed. When they came to the place called the Skull, they crucified him there, along with the criminals—one on his right, the other on his left. Jesus said, "Father, forgive them, for they do not know what they are doing." And they divided up his clothes by casting lots.

The people stood watching, and the rulers even sneered at him. They said, "He saved others; let him save himself if he is God's Messiah, the Chosen One."

The soldiers also mocked him. They offered him vinegar and said, "If you are the king of the Jews, save yourself." There was a written notice above him, which read: THIS IS THE KING OF THE JEWS.

The bleeding body of Jesus hung on the cross. He was in deep agony. In fact, in the Garden of Gethsemane, He prayed to the Father in Heaven 'If it is possible, remove this cup from me, yet not my will, but yours be done'.

Who were these criminals, hanging on either side of Jesus on the cross? According to the Book of Nicodemus, written in 4 A.D., the names of these two criminals were Dismas and Gestas. One of the criminals crucified with Christ recognized that He was not an ordinary man. That's the reason this thief accepted Jesus as his Saviour and expressed his faith in Him. So, this second thief made his request known to Jesus. He begged Jesus, "Remember me when You come into Your kingdom."

Jesus answered the repentant thief: "Truly I tell you, today you will be with Me in paradise." How lucky is this thief. The reason behind this blessing is that God is merciful and abundant in grace. To the dying man Jesus promised His forgiveness and eternal life. Here we see that, He is ready to pour out His grace to those who believe in Him.

He promised the man eternal life in paradise with Christ on the same day. There is no need for the thief to wait. The thief 's application was immediately approved. His faith earned him immediate residence in the Kingdom of God.

But, He has the authority and power to punish these evildoers. He has the power to call an army of angels to protect him. "Do you think I cannot call on my Father, and he will at once put at my disposal more than twelve legions of angels? But how then would the Scriptures be fulfilled that say it must happen in this way?" (Matthew 26:53-54)

Legion means 6,000 and twelve legions of angels means 12 X 6,000 = 72,000. But a massacre occurred in 2 Kings 19:35 through the prayer of Hezekiah, the King of Judah. It so happened that an enemy king invaded the kingdom of Hezekiah, the king of Judah. As an answer to the king's prayer an Angel came and killed 1,85,000 people. But the question is, if one Angel killed 1,85,000 people, how many people would 72,000 angels kill? 72,000, X 1,85,000

= 13,32,00,00,000 (13.32 billion – One billion means hundred crores) If this happened, the entire universe would have been destroyed. (In Jesus times, the estimated world population is 20 – 30 crores. This is equal to the population of Uttar Pradesh and Uttarakhand in India).

2.3 Message

For the wages of sin is death, but the gift of God is eternal life in Christ Jesus our Lord (Romans 6:23). Forgiveness in the first saying of Jesus is universal. The second word is immediately available to those who pray personally, as this thief did. Only Dr. Luke wrote about this second word. Jesus also revealed His divinity by opening heaven to the repentant sinner—how generous the Lord Jesus was to the one who only asked, "Remember me!" This love and forgiveness give hope and inspiration to those who seek salvation. Because if we open our hearts and turn to Him, pray to Him and accept His forgiveness, we too will be with Jesus Christ in the eternal world.

Many people were mocking Jesus who was hanging on the cross —the religious leaders, the authorities, the people, the soldiers, and the unrepentant thief. Jesus did not pay any attention to them. A good servant of the Lord said like this, "It doesn't matter what happens to you. But what is happening through you is important, which means - how you react to what is happening to you is very important." Based on your response your life i.e., your character can be determined.

Look at the Lord Jesus. No matter what others say or do, He did not change His nature and His purpose. He ignored the situation. The reason for him to be able to do so is His good virtues. He is full of truth and grace.

That is why He immediately responded with love to a repentant sinner's request. He gave courage and hope. When the thief said, 'Jesus, remember me when you come back.' Jesus replied, 'Today you will be with me in paradise'.

Will there be anyone or is there anyone who listens to a thief? This thief may not have seen any such person in his lifetime. Even though he was a thief, Jesus responded immediately and gave him eternal life. This is because, Jesus hears prayers like this.

"Two men went up to the temple to pray, one a Pharisee and the other a tax collector. The Pharisee stood and prayed about himself : 'God, I thank you that I am not like other people— robbers, evildoers, adulterers—or even like this tax collector. I fast twice a week and give a tenth of all I get."

But the tax collector stood at a distance. He would not

even look up to heaven, but beat his chest and said, 'God, have mercy on me, a sinner.' "I tell you that this man, rather than the other, went home justified before God. For all those who exalt themselves will be humbled, and those who humble themselves will be exalted." (Luke 18:10-14)

The thief prayed like this tax collector and was assured. 'Today you will be with me in paradise. There is no tomorrow in Jesus' calendar, but only today. The apostle James is talking about people who are thinking of making money by doing business. "Now listen, you who say, "Today or tomorrow we will go to this or that city, spend a year there, carry on business and make money." Why, you do not even know what will happen tomorrow. What is your life? You are a mist that appears for a little while and then vanishes. Instead, you ought to say, "If it is the Lord's will, we will live and do this or that." (James 4:13-15)

Today is the day of salvation. This is what the LORD says: "In the time of my favour I will answer you, and in the day of salvation I will help you; I will keep you and will make you to be a covenant for the people, to restore the land and to reassign its desolate inheritances (Isaiah 49:8)

Do not let your hearts be troubled. You believe in God; believe also in me. My Father's house has many rooms; if that were not so, would I have told you that I am going there to prepare a place for you? And if I go and prepare a place for you, I will come back and take you to be with me that you also may be where I am (John 14:1-3).

The thief took a last-minute opportunity to receive God's love and forgiveness, Jesus spoke not in anger, but with confidence and joy, promising him that he will be with Him in Paradise. Praise be to God.

The answer and response of Jesus is the same whether there is one person or ten or thousands in the congregation. "Do not be afraid, little flock, for your Father has been pleased to give you the kingdom." (Luke 12:32)

At that time, the Israelites were in slavery for 430 years. God delivered them through Moses and Aaron. Do you know how happily God brought them out that day? He brought out his people with rejoicing, his chosen ones with shouts of joy (Psalms 105:43).

It is with the same joy that today the Lord Jesus is redeeming His people by taking the pain and sufferings of death. That's why He came (Mark 10:45). The same thing, Paul also shared happily. I will very gladly not just gladly but very gladly spend everything I have for you and expend myself as well (2 Corinthians 12:15). So, believers and servants Worship the LORD with gladness; come before him with joyful songs (Psalms 100:2).

To save the human race and mankind from the wrath of God, Jesus came down to this world, and bore on His body the wrath of God that each of us should have experienced, from the first man on earth to the last man who will be on earth in the future.

God's forgiveness and grace are beyond our understanding. We are not qualified to talk about it. However, the Almighty God showed His grace to such unworthy people. "Yes, that's why the thief could get the Paradise, and we are going to see him. Jesus caught him in his last moments of death on the cross. He earned him.

Which of these two thieves are you? The one who rejects or the one who accepts, a neglecting person or a person who pays attention? Are you preparing for God's wrath or are you preparing for God's presence? The decision is yours my friend.

One of the criminals crucified with Christ recognized who Jesus was and expressed his faith in Him as Saviour. He received great salvation. Here we see the great grace of God, flowing through faith.

Jesus assures the dying man of His forgiveness and of eternal salvation. Jesus promised the man that on that day he would share eternal life with Christ in Paradise. The thief does not have to wait. His faith earned him immediate residence in the Kingdom of God.

Jesus was mocked. All mankind had mocked him. He was humiliated. Politicians, authorities, religious leaders - priests, high priests, military officers, soldiers, laymen, people, travelers, and finally even criminals mocked Jesus. They made him subject to the wretched punishment of death on the cross. But Jesus gladly accepted all this.

But who is this man? He is not a criminal, but the Saviour of the world. He did not commit any sin. He was sinless and rather deserved to forgive sins. He not only died, but rose again. He will come again for the second time. He conquered death. This man is the Lord Jesus. His kingdom is endless and eternal.

'Forgive them for they know not what they are doing'. After hearing this prayer, starting with the criminal on the right, all humanity is realizing the truth. This truth about receiving forgiveness, enjoying the salvation He freely grants. Praise be to God! May He be glorified for ever and ever.

2.4 Application

What is the best book to read in the world? To know yourself or read about yourself is the greatest book. In the past, I thought there were small mistakes and big mistakes in life. I thought, small ones are fine. I used to think that only for the big mistakes I need to be accountable to God. Later I learnt, there is no difference between small fire and big fire. What happens, if small fire and big fire are wrapped in different clothes? For small fire, it may take time, but it too will surely burn the cloth. Likewise, I realized small and big sin both are dangerous.

Even after accepting Christ as my Saviour, I did make some minor mistakes. As I was growing in my spiritual life, I realized that I am a saved sinner. There is no 'small fire or big fire'. Fire is fire. It burns everything. From then onwards, I have been trying to control myself.

The thief on the cross, in the last moments of his life 'read his book' and realized that he was a thief and a sinner. And it is a great blessing to know that the person hanging on the cross is no other than, the Creator and the Saviour of the world. One of the two thieves on the cross received this blessing.

What about you, my dear friend, just like those two

thieves, there are two type of thieves in this world. One is those who are caught. The second type is those who aren't yet. Undetected thieves think they are smart. But one day will come when no one can escape. On that day their sin will catch them. Before that day comes, know yourself. Confess your sins. And seek forgiveness from Jesus who is ready to receive your punishment. Accept Him as your Lord and Saviour, and receive eternal life and blessings.

2.5 Questions to be discussed

1. Have you observed or read your 'inner self'?

2. Which of the smaller or larger fires are you playing with?

3. Do you confess your fault or sin?

4. Do you know about life after your death?

5. Do you know how to earn eternal life?

3. HE SAID TO HER, "WOMAN, HERE IS YOUR SON," AND TO THE DISCIPLE, "HERE IS YOUR MOTHER". JOHN 19:26 - 27

Beloved John begins with the third word.

When Jesus saw his mother there, and the disciple whom he loved, standing nearby, he said to her, "Woman, here is your son," and to the disciple, "Here is your mother." From that time on, this disciple took her into his home (John 19:26-27).

Jesus was hanging on the cross. He had already spoken two words from the cross. First word for all – "Father, forgive them, for they do not know what they are doing."

The second word with the thief, "Truly, I tell you, today you will be with me in paradise."

What happened after these two events?

Luke writes that it was late afternoon and there had been darkness for three hours. The sun had disappeared. The veil of the temple was torn from top to bottom.

What about the father (earthly) and brothers of Jesus?

How involved was Joseph, the father in Jesus' life? Jesus was born by the Holy Spirit. Joseph was present at that time. On the eighth day he took Him to the temple. Fearing for his life, he took Jesus to Egypt as per the advice of the Angel. Heeding the advice of the same Angel, he returned to Nazareth with the boy Jesus. Finally, at the age of twelve, according to the tradition, they went to Jerusalem for the Passover festival. After that, there is no further mention of Joseph in the Scripture.

Perhaps he might have died before Jesus public ministry. If Joseph was alive, Joseph would have taken care of Mary.

Does Jesus have brothers and sisters? In fact, this passage indicates that the Jesus was the only child of his mother, Mary, because if he had biological brothers or sisters, they would have comforted her. But Jesus entrusted her care to the disciple John.

Mark 6:3 says, "Isn't this the carpenter? Isn't this Mary's son and the brother of James, Joseph, Judas and Simon? Aren't his sisters here with us?" According to this verse, Jesus has brothers and sisters.

At that time, the words brother and sister in Hebrew or

Aramaic also meant blood sibling, relative, or spiritual brother or sister. According to this, if James, Joseph, Judas, and Simon were also Mary's biological sons, why did they mention Jesus as "Mary's son" in singular form. Else, they might have said, "one of Mary's sons" in the plural form. Whatever it might be, Jesus thought of his mother when he was in the most terrible condition. Even at such a time, he made an arrangement for her.

3.1 Old Testament Prophecy

Jesus showed care and love towards His family, especially towards His mother. "Honour your parents," says the law. So, Jesus came into this world to fulfil the law. "Honour your father and your mother, so that you may live long in the land the LORD your God is giving you" (Exodus 20:12).

3.2 Fulfillment in the New Testament

John writes about the soldiers sharing Jesus' clothes. Thus, they fulfilled the prophecy of Psalms 22:18. There are now three Marys near the cross of Jesus. One is Mary, the mother, secondly Mary the wife of Cleophas and thirdly Mary Magdalene. And some women were standing nearby.

Then Jesus looked at his mother and said these words: "Mother, behold your son." Then he said to his disciple John,

"Here is your mother."

This third word "The Word of Relationship" refers to the "relationship" Jesus entrusts his mother Mary to the care of "the disciple John whom he loved".

From here, his dear mother did not let go of her son until Jesus was laid in the tomb. While witnessing this scene, Mary may have remembered the prophecy given by the prophet Simeon about 33 years ago.

Now there was a man in Jerusalem called Simeon, who was righteous and devout. He was waiting for the consolation of Israel, and the Holy Spirit was on him. It had been revealed to him by the Holy Spirit that he would not die before he had seen the Lord's Messiah. Moved by the Spirit, he went into the temple courts. When the parents brought in the child Jesus to do for him what the custom of the Law required, Simeon took Him in his arms and praised God, saying: "Sovereign Lord, as you have promised, you may now dismiss your servant in peace.

For my eyes have seen your salvation, which you have prepared in the sight of all nations: a light for revelation to the Gentiles, and the glory of your people Israel." The child's father and mother marveled at what was said about Him. Then

Simeon blessed them and said to Mary, His mother: "This child is destined to cause the falling and rising of many in Israel, and to be a sign that will be spoken against, so that the thoughts of many hearts will be revealed. And a sword will pierce your own soul too" (Luke 2:25-35).

Perhaps mother Mary, when she saw the blood-stained body of Jesus, remembered that the prophecy Simeon had said on that day was fulfilled today.

Jesus, looking down from the cross, may still be concerned about his mother's earthly needs, the arrangements he had to make as her son. None of his brothers were there to look after her, even if they were at home He had to fulfil His duty as the eldest son. So, Jesus entrusted this work to the Apostle John. Here we clearly see the humanity of Christ.

3.3 Message

Not only Bible, but all religious books say that everyone should respect their parents. What are the things children owe to their parents? Remember what your parents did for you. Your mother carried nine months in the womb, gave birth to you. Do you know how hard it was to raise you up? Do you know how much care your health was taken care of? Do you know how much they had paid and how much sweat they had shed and earned money for your studies and your fees? Do you know how much they have struggled when you had been sick or suffered any injury? Do you know how depressed they had been and how much they had suffered when you were destroying yourself with bad habits? You might have remembered how they had led you in the right way spiritually? In a gist, they risked their lives and gave us everything.

In our Indian tradition, (love marriages are different) it is the parents who look for the life partner, bring the proposal, decide for the marriage and arrange the marriage at a huge expense or within their means. After being brought up and getting married in this way, if the son bids farewell to his parents, what is to become of their fate? How do they feel? What would be their condition in old age? Who will take care of them? Who should help them?

The Bible is very deep, holy and mysterious. It is the glory of God to conceal a matter; to search out a matter is the glory of kings (Proverbs 25:2). So, we have to investigate this deeply.

Three different things are written in the Bible.

1. What does it mean to leave one's father and mother after marriage and cling to one's wife? What is the meaning of Genesis 2:24?

2. The first of the Ten Commandments God gave to the people of Israel was, honour your father and your mother, so that you may live long in the land the LORD your God is giving you. (Exodus 20:12). Apostle Paul also says that, if you respect your parents, you will enjoy a long and healthy life. Children, obey your parents in the Lord, for this is the right thing to do. "Honour your father and mother"—which is the first commandment with a promise— "so that it may go well with you and that you may enjoy long life on the earth (Ephesians 6:1-3). What is the meaning of this?

3. If anyone comes to me and does not hate father and mother, wife and children, brothers and sisters—yes, even their own life—such a person cannot be my disciple. And whoever does not carry their cross and follow me cannot be my disciple. What does Luke 14:26-27 mean?

Three answers -

1. Husband and wife should prefer each other for the sake of marital relationship. What does it mean to leave one's father and mother after marriage and cling to one's wife? (Genesis 2:24). Because of this verse, some people teach that after marriage, wife is priority and the parents can be left behind. Others follow it. Is this true?

The Bible is God's Word. It is more valuable than gold and diamonds. It reveals the mind of God to us. So, it is important to study the Bible well and know what it says about the relationships and responsibilities of children and parents. The same should be followed.

For example, children leave their parents at home while they go to school. After school, they run and hug their parents. Due to a reason, a necessity, the child leaves the parents and stays in school for some time. Also, husbands and wives need some time to spend alone and peaceful in order to perform their marital responsibility. If separated, parents should be separated only for this cause.

The son/daughter should respect their parents and take care of them. This should be reciprocated by the husband and wife for each other's parents. Everyone calls their spouse's parents aunt (mother-in-law) and uncle (father-in-law). What does it mean? According to law, the parents of the wife are also the parents of the husband. Husband's parents also become wife's parents.

A family which understands and practices in this way is a model family and is like MINI HEAVEN.

2. Priority should be given to the parents for giving birth, rearing and making them able for adulthood (Exodus 20:12, Ephesians 6:1-3)

Every family member should know how to serve parents and how to pay off their debts. In the Old Testament, David was running for his life, ignorant of where to hide. Saul, the king of Israel, was trying to kill him.

Even in times of danger David supported his parents and siblings. The Word says that he preserved them. (1 Samuel 22:1- 2)

Similarly, in the New Testament Apostle Paul encourages Timothy by questioning him. He must manage his own family well and see that his children obey him, and he must do so in a manner worthy of full respect. How shall a man rule the church of God if he does not know his own household? Husband should rule, protect and take good care of the family.

Give proper recognition to those widows who are really in need. But if a widow has children or grandchildren, first of all, they should learn to put their religion into practice by caring for their own family and so repaying their parents and grandparents, for this is pleasing to God. (1 Timothy 3:4, 5:3-4).

Religion that God our Father accepts as pure and faultless is this: to look after orphans and widows in their distress and to keep oneself from being polluted by the world (James 1:27).

There was a servant who served the Lord all his life in two Telugu states. He was from a Brahmin family and became a Christian. His name is R. R. K. Murthy, he had said, "A family is a small church and a church is a big family." This is absolute truth. This should be observed and followed by all, especially God's servants.

3. First priority should be given to God who gave life and saved us. God is the creator. He first loved us. And He loved perfectly. He sacrificed His life for us and bore the penalty of our sins. He died for us. Likewise, we should Love the Lord with all our heart and with all our soul and with all our mind and with all our strength. (Mark 12:30, Luke 14:26-27)

Do not take a verse off the Bible and interpret it. The verses before and after it should also be read. Related verses are also found throughout the Bible. They should be searched, read, understood and interpreted together.

Jesus made arrangements for his mother. This service is acceptable. Even though, He was hanging on the cross and bleeding, He remembered His mother and entrusted John with the responsibility of caring for her. Jesus Christ on the cross proclaimed the cure for all fallen and unhealthy human relationships. He had obeyed. This is a good example. Jesus respected his mother, took care of her and also protected her. The disciples of Jesus should also follow in his footsteps!!!

3.4 Application

I lost my father when I was young. We are five siblings. My mother brought us up with lot of hardships. We looked after our mother very gratefully. I was the first person in our family to know Jesus Christ as my Lord and Saviour. That's why my mother used to fight with me in the first few days. It was because she felt that I had accepted a foreign god and a low caste god. My mother observed my changed life closely for six months. After that she testified that the God you are worshiping is the true God. She also accepted Lord Jesus as her personal Saviour.

My marriage to Mary, the first daughter of Pastor Lavu Apparao, took place in 1981. We have two children, Tabitha and Daniel, both of them are married, I have four grandchildren. My mother went to be with the Lord at the age of 85.

We as husband and wife showed our love and gratitude to our parents on both sides. As a token of thankfulness, we gave our parents the experience of flying in air. This may not be a great thing to some. But for us who come from a poor family, this is a great thing. However, no matter how much is done for the parents, it is still less.

We should obey our parents when we are under their care. After marriage, we should love, respect and protect our parents in every area. Both husband and wife should serve their parents with care. Everyone should repay their parents with love and care for the services they have shown us from conception to the end of our lives.

Thereafter, there will be peace, joy and happiness in the family. Every family should be like a little heaven. The example Jesus' put forth of fulfilling family responsibilities is great. This is what each of us, as His disciples should always follow. Then only God will receive the glory.

He said to her, "Woman, here is your son," and to the disciple, "Here is your mother." From that time on, this disciple took her into his home.

3.5 Questions to be discussed

1. Do you respect and obey your parents?

2. Are you reciprocating your relationship with your parents after your marriage?

3. Do you treat your spouse's parents equally with love?

4. Are you teaching your children to love and respect elders?

5. What can you do to make your children love you even more than you loved your parents?

4. "MY GOD, MY GOD, WHY HAVE YOU FORSAKEN ME". MARK 15:34

The chief priests, scribes and others had been insulting Jesus saying, "You who would destroy the temple and rebuild it in three days,   save yourself, and come down from the cross!" , In fact Jesus came not to save Himself not to escape the cross but to seek and save the lost by carrying the cross.

According to the gospel of Mark, Jesus was crucified at the third hour and He spoke the fourth word at ninth hour. What are these timings? Mark 15.26,34.

The 3rd hour of the day (about 3 hours after sunrise), roughly 9.00am our time. The 9th hour of the day (about 9 hours after sunrise), roughly 3.00pm our time. This means that almost six hours, Jesus had been hanging, experiencing the unimaginable and unexplainable pain on the cross. Matthew wrote that from the sixth hour there was darkness over all the land until the ninth hour- which means the darkness was for three hours from 12oo noon until 3oo pm.

At this moment, Jesus cried unto God in a loud voice, *"Eloi, Eloi, lema sabachthani?"* (which means "My God, my God, why have you forsaken me?") (Mark 15:34).

About three in the afternoon Jesus cried out in a loud voice, *"Eli, Eli, lema sabachthani?"* (Matthew 27:46) What is the difference between the words of the evangelists Matthew and Mark? Matthew said, Eli Eli Lama Sabachthani. The reason is that Matthew wrote his book to the Jews. The official language of the Jews is Hebrew. Mark wrote Eloi Eloi in Aramaic, the common language of the day. But the meaning is the same, said B.I Premaiah, an old testament teacher.

4.1 Old Testament prophecy

This is the only word that appears in more than one gospel. The psalmist prophesied these words. My God, my God, why have you forsaken me? Why are you so far from saving me, so far from my cries of anguish? (Psalms 22.1) This is a Psalm written by David. Perhaps King Saul was chasing to kill him. We don't know how far he had walked, how far he had run, what did he eat, where he had slept. God, you have chosen me, you have seen my innermost being, you said "I will make you king for generations". May be he was lamenting or questioning his personal situation, saying "Why did you leave me now?"

But we must see these words in the context in which Psalms 22 was written. In the whole psalm, whom do these words refer to, David or Jesus or someone else! So, David said it. And the word declares that Jesus is the son of David. When we consider these

words we need to observe. Even if hardships and sufferings come, even if everyone thinks that they have left us, we must endure with patience. But should not be disappointed. And do not leave the eternal God of refuge.

Anyway, it's only a matter of time for realization. Readers should realize that, and we know that in all things God works for the good of those who love Him, who have been called according to His purpose (Romans 8:28).

But this word was also fulfilled in the life of Jesus. He fulfilled it. As soon as He said this, the religious leaders and people around the cross mistakenly thought that He was calling Elijah for help.

According to this word, some consider that the Father left the Son completely. From another point of view, when Jesus took the sins of all mankind upon Himself, God the Father turned His face away from His Son. Perhaps this last view is true. God is holy and pure and has holy eyes which are too pure to look on evil (Habakkuk 1:13).

It is a cry of true human nature. The cry of Jesus, who alone bears the burden of the sins of the world. He was abandoned by his friends, the disciples. He was being punished by His enemies. Even God, the ever-present Father, has finally abandoned Him. It is an unbearable anguish. That is why Jesus cried out.

The scribes and Pharisees asked Him to come down from the cross, and challenged Him to save Himself. But Jesus came to this world not to save Himself. Not to come down from the cross. He had explained it before, telling them of the reason why He came, what kind of hardships He would face and how eventually He was going to die. The contents of the 22nd psalm indicates that, Jesus was appointed to experience all this suffering in His life. For, He is our Passover Lamb (1 Corinthians 5:7).

The deepest love and eternal love for God the Father is the evidence of perfect sacrifice. However, as soon as His Father let go of His hand, Jesus cried out. My God, my God, why have you forsaken me?

Never before had the Father forsaken His Son except at this occasion. A time is coming and in fact, has come when you will be scattered, each to your own home. You will leave Me all alone. Yet I am not alone, for my Father is with Me. He told them, "I and the Father are one." But, if I do judge, My decisions are true, because I am not alone. I stand with the Father, who sent Me (John 16:32, 10:30, 8:16).

4.2 Fulfillment in the New Testament

According to Jewish time it is ninth hour (Mark 15:34 says it is three hours) when Jesus cried out with a loud voice, *"Eli, Eli, lama sabachtani*?" meaning, "My God, my God, why have you forsaken me? (Matthew 27:46).

The first three gospels described this horrific scene of the crucifixion - agony in the Garden of Gethsemane, trial before the Sanhedrin, abandonment of the disciples, vile mockery and torture while suffering all of it alone on the cross, the whole body is ploughed like furrows (Psalms 129:3). Suffering, darkness upon the earth, the holy eyes of the Father turning away from Him all of this combined led Jesus to utter this fourth word, My God, my God, why have you forsaken me? (Matthew 27:46-51 Mark 15:33- 38). This word is called the cross within the cross by biblical scholars. The reason is Jesus's pain and sufferings reached the climax during the fourth word.

Jesus had already spoken the first three words - 'forgiveness'; 'Salvation' 'right relationship'. After this third word there is a pause of about three hours. Jesus experienced this agony, unable to bear the pain of being separated from the Father, Jesus thus cried out 'Why did you leave Me alone'?

Jesus enjoyed the most intimate fellowship with the Father throughout His life, and especially before He came into this world. He made this clear in His high priestly prayer.

Before the foundation of the world, Jesus was with the Father in glory and majesty. God the Father loved Jesus the Son before the foundation of the world. First the Father and then everything that the Father has, belongs to Jesus, the Son (Numbers 18:20, Luke 15:31). Jesus, the Son, and the Holy Father, are united. The Son is in the Father and the Father is in the Son. The Father sent Jesus into this world. Jesus came and was sent to this world not only to show the glory of the Father to the world but also to give that glory to those who received Him. These hardships are only temporary. Jesus knew that He was going to the Father. So Jesus said, "When you have lifted up the Son of Man, then you will know that I am He and that I do nothing on my own but speak just what the Father has taught me. He that sent me is with me. He said that He never left me alone as I always do the work which pleases Him

(John 8:16, 28,39, 17:5,10,11,20,24).

Despite all the above experiences, Jesus prayed twice to remove this bowl - once when the Greeks came to see Him and again the second time in the Garden of Gethsemane. ? No, it was for this very reason I came to this hour." (John 12:27) "Now my soul is troubled, and what shall I say? Father, save me from this hour."

The second word is in the Garden of Gethsemane. Jesus yielded His will to the Father saying, "Father, if you are willing, take this cup from me; yet not my will, but yours be done" (Luke 22:42).

4.3 Message

Lord Jesus is divine man. He showed divine power in the form of God. We know that God does not listen to sinners. He listens to the godly person who does his will. Nobody has ever heard of opening the eyes of a man born blind. If this man were not from God, he could do nothing (John 9:31-33).

Some of the Pharisees said, "This man is not from God, for he does not keep the Sabbath." Well, let's think so for a while. "How can a sinner perform such signs?" (John 9:16) There is no answer to this question. So, what we need to realize is that, Jesus is the embodiment of the invisible God. He is holy. All things are possible with Him.

But He is also fully human. He is tired, hungry, thirsty, sleepy, happy, angry. Like everyone else, he has the fear of death. He prayed thrice to avoid this. Finally, He surrendered Himself saying - Father, let thy will be done.

Like Jacob, we all fear death when we face it. Jacob, Abraham's grandson, fearing 'death' from his brother, sent his family members ahead of him in groups to pacify his brother, and he himself was left alone on the banks of the river Jabbok (Genesis 32:8,24). This was Jacob's fear of death.

Jesus' fourth word is a prophecy of Psalms 22, so His cry from the cross reminds of Jacob's cry. It also reminds us of all the people of darkness residing in the shadows of death. In this psalm, in the days when there was no knowledge of the cross, David gave a wonderful prophecy of the crucifixion of the Messiah.

"They pierce my hands and my feet. All my bones are on display". The Psalm continues: " They divide my clothes among them and cast lots for my garment" (Psalms 22:16-18).

There will never be a more terrible moment in the history of mankind. It has not come and will not come. Jesus incarnated for our salvation and was crucified. He suffered the terrible punishment of sin, the severity of it, on the cross. Like the fury of sin, the waves of the sea are about to overwhelm Jesus. Sometimes it looks like evil is going to win. But it's not the reality. It is only for a few moments. That is why Jesus said to the people who came with Judas Iscariot, "This is your hour" (Luke 22:53). The burden of mankind's sin appears to overcome our Saviour the 'Son of Man' for a moment. But it is never possible.

In order for Jesus to save us, should this not happen? Most assuredly, it should. It was through the cross that His Father's plan of salvation was to be fulfilled (Ephesians 1:7-10). Through His death there is redemption of mankind. "This is good, and pleasing to God our Saviour, who wants all people to be saved and to come to a knowledge of the truth. For there is one God and one mediator between God and mankind, the man Christ Jesus, who gave himself as a ransom for all people" (1 Timothy 2:3-6). "He Himself bore our sins in His body on the cross, so that we might die to sins and live for righteousness; by His wounds you have been healed" (1 Peter 2:24). He had to bear the weight of our sins so that we may be freed from our sin and live righteously.

4.4 Application

In my life too, I had to say - God, why have you forsaken me? On 24 April, 2021 I was admitted to the hospital with Covid. After nine days of struggle, I was healed by the grace of God and reached home. But by the time I got home my wife Mary was also infected with covid. We travelled in the ambulance to the hospitals in Indore for one whole day. There was not even one bed available to admit my wife in the hospital. The same ambulance brought her home in the evening. The same day, late at night, I got a phone call from the hospital that a bed was vacant. We admitted her the same night in the hospital. Treatment was given for nine days in the same hospital. Each day they say, she will get better and will be discharged, but they keep extending the date. Finally we got fed up and forcefully got her discharged and admitted to the hospital where I was first admitted. After four days, my wife left me and entered the heavenly home on 17th May 2021. She had suffered a cardiac arrest. Perhaps a similar question could be asked, O God, why have you made me lonely? Why did you take my wife?

The pain of losing my beloved wife on one hand and the pressure of relatives on the other hand, who do not know the Lord added on to the grief. "What will you gain if you remain there, return to the south i.e. Hyderabad", they said. I thought, I don't know what to do. I am lonely. But my inner soul said that this time will prevail only for a while. My dear Lord Jesus, who loved me and gave His life for me, comforted me, empowered me and gave me the strength to face the reality. It means that one day everyone has to leave this world. I extend many praises to my Jesus who gave me new strength to continue in this ministry.

Jesus is our great example in all things. He was alone on the cross, His friends had abandoned him and even His heavenly Father had left Him. Why did God have to leave? It is so because at this very moment God the Father laid the sins of the world on His Son. Jesus took the punishment of entire world's sins. "He who had no sin, was made sin for us" (2 Corinthians 5:21). God's holy eyes cannot behold evil, so the Father in heaven left His beloved Son alone. Jesus is the Lamb of God that takes away the sin of the world. No one can redeem the life of another or give to God a ransom for them. The ransom for a life is costly, no payment is ever enough.

For anyone to live on forever, so that they should not see decay, says in Psalms 49:7-9. The only power and person to atone for universal sin is Jesus. Because He is without any sin, He is holy. So, He is worthy to pay the ransom for many. This price

He offered is not silver and gold but His life itself (Matthew 20:28).

Though Jesus had done no violence, nor was any deceit in his mouth, yet it was the LORD's will to crush him. He offered Himself as an offering for sin (Isaiah 53:9-10). Therefore, God the Father allowed Jesus to fulfil the mission of saving the world. He left Him alone.

Even the disciples, in order to proclaim the way of salvation in today's world, should follow the Master's way. Jesus clearly told his followers –"If anyone comes to me and does not hate father and mother, wife and children, brothers and sisters—yes, if they don't hate even their own lives—such a person cannot be my disciple. And whoever does not carry their cross and follow me cannot be my disciple" (Luke 14:26-27). Not only that, "Blessed are those who are persecuted because of righteousness, for theirs is the kingdom of heaven. Blessed are you when people insult you, persecute you and falsely say all kinds of evil against you because of me. Rejoice and be glad, because great is your reward in heaven, for in the same way they persecuted the prophets who were before you" (Matthew 5:10-12).

These passages reminds the cost of discipleship. Every disciple has to lay down his life as a living sacrifice. The best example is a candle which has to be consumed itself in order to give light. No gain without pain.

"I have told you these things, so that in Me you may have peace. In this world you will have trouble. But take heart! I have overcome the world" (John 16:33). For it has been granted to you on behalf of Christ not only to believe in Him, but also to suffer for Him (Philippians 1:29). Suffering for Jesus is both a privilege and a responsibility. What do you say?

Suffering is a part of life. Look at the candle, it must dissolve itself to give light. No result comes without effort. NO PAIN NO GAIN. There is no crown without the cross. In Christ, suffering and death are not the last words, they are the first words and the beginning of the resurrection. It is because Jesus had conquered death, He had won victory over death.

Jesus cried out in a loud voice, *"Eloi, Eloi, lema sabachthani?"* - My God, my God, why have you forsaken me? (Mark 15:34).

4.5 Questions to be discussed

1. Why would the righteous experience more trouble... How would you explain?

2.   If none is by your side, how would you face loneliness?

3.   If you face persecutions for witnessing to the name of the
     Lord Jesus, how would you respond?

4.   How would you explain that suffering and death are not
     the last words in a Christian's life?

5. "I AM THIRSTY". JOHN 19:28

Jesus is Omniscient. He knows the thoughts of the people (Matt 12.25, Luke 9.47), He knows the hypocrisy of the people (Mark 12.15), He knows what is going to happen to Him (John 18.4) and He knows that His time on the earth is going to complete (John 13.1). Jesus knows that all the scriptures must fulfill in His life and through His life.

Jesus, again knowing that all was now finished, said this fifth word (to fulfill the Scripture), "I thirst." John 19.28

The fifth word spoken on the cross was "I thirst" (John 19:28).

5.1 Old Testament Prophecy

The fifth word spoken by Jesus was written by the disciple John in the gospel of John 19:28 as the fulfillment of the prophecy written in Psalms 69. "They put gall in my food and gave me vinegar for my thirst" (Psalms 69:21). Later, knowing that everything had been finished, Jesus said, "I am thirsty", so that

Scripture would be fulfilled.

This is the fulfillment of Psalm 69 in which David says, "Answer me LORD, out of the goodness of Your love; in Your great mercy turn to me. Do not hide Your face from Your servant; answer me quickly for I am in trouble.

Come near and rescue me; deliver me because of my foes. You know I am scorned, disgraced and shamed; all my enemies are before you. Scorn has broken my heart and has left me helpless; I looked for sympathy but there was none; I looked for comforters but I found none. They put gall in my food and gave me vinegar for my thirst" (Psalms 69:16-21).

Another time David also prophesied, "My mouth is dried up like a potsherd, and my tongue sticks to the roof of my mouth; you lay me in the dust of death. Dogs surround me, a pack of villains encircle me; they pierce my hands and my feet. All my bones are on display; people stare at me and gloat over me. They divide my clothes among them and cast lots for my garment. But you LORD, do not be far from me. You are my strength; come quickly to help me" (Psalms 22:15-19).

God invites His people through the prophet Isaiah, "Come, all you who are thirsty, come to the waters; and you who have no money, come, buy and eat! Come, buy wine and milk without money and without cost. Why spend money on what is not bread and your labour on what does not satisfy? Listen, listen to me, and eat what is good, and you will delight in the richest of fare. Give ear and come to me; listen, that you may live. I will make an everlasting covenant with you, my faithful love promised to David" (Isaiah 55:1-3).

5.2 Fulfillment in the New Testament

Jesus said, "I thirst" (John 19:28). This word can be called "The Word of Distress". In love, He bore all the pain, suffering, sin, and curse for us. The wages of sin is death, which He paid on His body, for this the Lord Jesus was 'thirsty'.

In John 4, He was thirsty at the well. He may have meant to quench the spiritual thirst of the Samaritan woman. That is why Jesus said, "I am thirsty".

Jesus was sitting by the well tired. A Samaritan woman came to the same well to draw water. While Jesus was conversing with her, the disciples brought food. They said, "Teacher, eat." But He said, "I have food to eat that you know nothing about." The disciples said to one another, "Could someone have brought Him anything to eat?" "My food," said Jesus, "is to do the will of Him who sent Me and to finish His work."

When Jesus met the Samaritan woman at the well, He asked for a drink to quench His thirst. After asking for a "drink," He replied to the woman, "Everyone who drinks this water will be thirsty again, but whoever drinks the water I give them will never thirst. Indeed, the water I give them will become in them a spring of water welling up to eternal life" (John 4:7, 13-14). This passage indicates that there is more value than just physical thirst. This spring must gradually become a stream.

Jesus went to the town of Samaria to offer his 'living water'. He found a representative and sold the water to all the villagers (John 4). Jesus is the Almighty God. He has the skill to sell His product. He revealed himself step by step. He also informed the quality of his product. Who is He? Creator, Saviour of the world. Gradually she realized: First a Jew – then a Prophet – later Messiah / Christ – finally Savior of the world.

1. Jesus as a Jew

The Samaritan woman came to the well to draw water. Jesus said to her, "Will you give Me a drink."

The Samaritan woman said to Him, "You are a Jew and I am a Samaritan woman. How can You ask me for a drink?" (John 4:7,9) Samaritans are mixed race so Jews do not associate with them. Jesus came to this world not for the healthy. He came into this world to give more than we ask or expect.

Donor – Donation:

Who or what is great? The 'gift' or the 'giver'!!! Jesus said to her, "If you knew the gift of God (donation) and who (donor) it is that asks you for a drink, you would have asked Him and He would have given you living water" (John 4:10).

Jesus is the Living water. He said to her, "Everyone who drinks this water will be thirsty again, but whoever drinks the water I give them will never thirst. Indeed, the water I give them will become in them a spring of water welling up to eternal life" (John 4:13- 14).

2. Jesus as a prophet

"Sir," the woman said, "I can see that you are a prophet" (John 4:19). Because, Jesus revealed the secrets of her heart.

3. Jesus the Messiah/Christ the Anointed One, the Chosen One

The woman said, "I know that Messiah" (called Christ)" is coming. When He comes, He will explain everything to us." Then Jesus introduced Himself," I, the one speaking to you—

I am He." He revealed His existence. During the conversation, He surely had been in commoner's dress. That is why He was not recognized at first but Jesus revealed Himself gradually. This revelation was promptly appreciated by the woman and immediately she recognized His identity as the Messiah. "Come, meet this man, he knew everything I had ever done and He has told me all about it. Could this be the Messiah?" (John4:25-26,29 says, she proclaimed to the entire town. (In Telugu translation, it's written as village; in English, it's written as town or city; in Hindi, it's written as Nagar).

Jesus is the Saviour of the world. Because of her testimony, there was a change in all the villagers. They said to the woman, "We don't just believe because of what you have said; now we have heard for ourselves, we personally know that this man really is the Saviour of the world." (John 4:42)

Jesus' food and drink were to do only the Father's will: "My food," said Jesus, "is to do the will of Him who sent Me and to finish His work" (John 4:34). Jesus was 'asking for a drink' yet offered 'Living waters'. By asking for a drink, He invited people to ask for the Living water He wanted to give them.

Jesus gave the woman living water. She left the water pot and invited everyone in the village to drink the living water she had experienced. It was as if she had adopted her village.

Who is Jesus?

He is the one who leads us to living waters.

Jesus invites the thirsty. On the last and greatest day of the festival, Jesus stood and said in a loud voice, "Let anyone who is thirsty come to me and drink. Whoever believes in me, as Scripture has said, rivers of living water will flow from within them." By this he meant the Spirit, whom those who believed in him were to receive later. Up to that time the Spirit had not been given, since Jesus had not yet been glorified. (John 7:37-39).

Even when Jesus was thirsty, He gave food and quenched the thirst of millions of Israelites in their wilderness journey. On this matter, confessing his own sins and the sins of all the people in the country, Nehemiah said, "They refused to listen and failed to remember the miracles you performed among them. They became stiff-necked and in their rebellion appointed a leader in order to return to their slavery. But you are a forgiving God, gracious and compassionate, slow to anger and abounding in love" (Nehemiah 9:17).

To quench the thirst of the millions of Israelites wandering in the desert, He made living waters flow from the rock. The first time He told, strike the rock (Exodus 17:6). That rock was Christ (1 Corinthians 10:4). Second time He said, to speak with the rock.

But Moses struck the rock the second time as well. As a result, He could not enter the land flowing with milk and honey (Numbers 20:8-12). What we need to understand about the rock and Moses is that the rock needs to be struck only once i.e. Jesus was crucified on the cross for our sins only once... and then we must speak, which means we need to pray. Ask for His help. He will surely help. If we strike again, that means, if we sin again, He will not be crucified again. But He punishes – be aware of it.

On that same day the LORD told Moses, "Go up into the Abarim Range to Mount Nebo in Moab, across from Jericho, and view Canaan, the land I am giving the Israelites as their own possession. There on the mountain that you have climbed you will die and be gathered to your people, just as your brother Aaron died on Mount Hor and was gathered to his people. This is because both of you broke faith with Me in the presence of the Israelites at the waters of Meribah-Kadesh in the Desert of Zin and did not uphold My holiness among the Israelites. Therefore, you will see the land only from a distance; you will not enter the land I am giving to the people of Israel" (Deuteronomy 32:48-52). Thus we see in the life of Moses, the meekest man on the earth, was not exceptional.

However, the death of Jesus is for everyone who is far away from Him. Here all the sins of the world fell upon Him. Now He was physically shocked with wounds from scourging, crowning with thorns, and walking through the streets of Jerusalem to Golgotha, where His blood drenched the ground. Finally after reaching the hill of Calvary, Jesus was hung upon the cross. His pain, sufferings and agonies had reached the peak. Hence he cried.

On the cross, Jesus thirsted for the living water. It is physical and spiritual thirst (John 7:38,39). Physical thirst:

The night before, Jesus spent without sleep. After the last supper, He went to the Garden of Gethsemane. He prayed to the Father in heaven. Jesus asked Him to remove the cup from Him. But He prayed, not My will but Your will be done. In the end, Jesus came to the conclusion that the father's silence meant that He had to drink from the 'cup'. When the time was right, Judas Iscariot came with his group. Jesus was arrested.

Firstly, they brought Him to the home of an unofficial priest named Annas. This Annas was Caiaphas' uncle. Then they took him to Caiaphas, the high priest. It was he who led

Jesus to the Sanhedrin, the governing body. After the trials of the religious leaders resulting in convictions, the politician led Jesus to the governor and judge, Pilate.

By then, it was morning. In other words, Jesus was led here and there throughout the night. He couldn't sleep.

Jesus was first questioned by Pilate. He then sent Him to Herod in Galilee. After He arrived from Galilee, Pilate took some more time.

Jesus was insulted, people had spat on His face, he was scourged (perhaps 39 times which was the usual order in those days), and a crown of thorn was placed on His head. He must have bled a lot already. Finally, at 9 o'clock in the morning, Jesus was crucified. At 12 noon Jesus spoke the first three words- Forgive them for they do not know what they are doing. Today you will be with me in paradise. To the mother He said, 'Behold thy son' and to the disciple whom he entrusted His mother he said, 'Behold thy mother'. After that, as if by divine decree, it had turned pitch black for three hours. The sun had disappeared. At this time, the veil of the temple was torn in two from top to bottom. Approximately at that time, Jesus had uttered the fourth word. 'My God, my God, why have you forsaken me'?

From the time Jesus spoke the first word, He had been hanging on the cross for over six hours with the bleeding body. It was nine o'clock in the morning when they crucified him (Mark 15:25). So, by the time the three hours of darkness had passed away, He had been hanging on the cross for a total of six hours. Naturally the water in his body had evaporated. Streams of blood had flown out of His body. It was then that He needed water. The thirst of Jesus, the living water, must be quenched. Now was the time for Him to ask for water.

Thirst in a spiritual sense

Jesus thirsted for love. He was also waiting for the love of His disciples. He is thirsty to give eternal life to all mankind. In the same way, Jesus thirsted for His Father's love. And in this terrible pain, God the Father left Him helpless. This great work of sacrifice must now be accomplished by the Lord Jesus himself.

Jesus told His disciples in the fourth chapter of John that His food and drink was to do the will of the Father who had sent Him. He preached and practiced the will of the Father.

After that, knowing that all things had been fulfilled according to the scriptures, Jesus said, "I thirst" (John 19:28).

5.3 Message

The Lord Jesus' thirst was primarily to fulfil the will of the Father in heaven. He is ever thirsty to please His Father. Everyone must be saved and have an experience of the truth. All who believe in Jesus as Lord and the Father who had sent Him are united in spirit to serve with one vision and one spirit.

"Come, everyone who is thirsty, come to the waters; and you without money, come, buy, and eat! Come, buy wine and milk without money and without cost!   (Isaiah 55:1)

Blessed are those who hunger for righteousness, for they will be satisfied. (Matthew 5:6)

Now, even in this 21st century, the Lord Jesus is telling you that he is 'thirsty'. So, to fulfill Jesus' thirsty, one should avoid the following five things according to 1 Peter 2:1

1. all evil

2. all deceit

3. all hypocrisy

4. all envy

5. all slander

Another five things which need to be observed and followed – 1. You are a new born baby, 2. You need pure milk which is the Word of God, 3. This milk should be desired forever, 4. After that as you grow take strong food Hebrews 5:12-14, 5. As a result grow in the salvation and change into the likenss of Christ Gal 4:19.

Salvation is related to three tenses.

1.1 Need to have salvation – past tense, deliverance from sin (Eph 2:5) After receiving salvation need to be delivered from the penalty of sin. Being justified – Justification.

1.2 Continue in salvation – present tense, to be delivered from the power of sin (1 Peter 2:1-2, Phil 2:12)

To continue in salvation, need to be delivered from the power of sin. Must be holy. Purification / Sanctification.

1.3 Being continue in salvation – future tense, to be delivered from the presence of sin (Rom 13:11)

To come out of the presence of sin. Glorification.

After that you need to share your experience with the entire mankind. Then only Jesus thirst will be quenched.

What are the ways and means to quench the 'thirst' of

Jesus Christ today ?

A person is refreshed when 'thirst' is quenched. Refresh means freshness or calmness. If you quench the thirst of a thirsty person it means you have filled him. Given him peace and calmness. You will be surely rewarded for this.

1. Accept the invitation of the Lord Jesus. If anyone is afflicted, let him come to me and be healed. He had said aloud that whoever believes in Him will have rivers of life flowing out of his belly, just as the scripture says. (John 7:37-38)

2. Accept Jesus Christ as your Lord and Saviour, confess your sins, receive the forgiveness of the Lord and rejoice in His presence as a child of God. (Luke 15:10, Acts 3:19-20, John 1:12, Luke 18:14, 1Corinthians 3:16)

3. Meet the minimum needs of those around you as much as possible (Matthew 25:37). The Lord Jesus said that if you give a small glass of water in the name of the Lord Jesus, you will surely receive its reward (Matthew 10:42, Matthew 9:41).

4. Finishing well is so important in the Christian life. The wine at Cana's wedding feast was more delicious at the end than at the beginning (John 2:7).

5. Have Godly friends. Paul was a prisoner for the Gospel. When the ship was stopped in the midst of journey, he was allowed to go to his friends and consult (refresh) them. (Acts 27:3, 1 cor 16:17-18, 2 Tim 1:15-17, Phil 1:7-20)

6. Follow the Sabbath. Work hard for five/six days and complete your work. Worship God in spirit and truth and take rest on the Lord's day (Exodus 23:12). Spend quality time with family and turn off cell phones.

7. Love others with joy (2 Corinthians 7:13)

8. Walk with God by the still waters (Psalms 23.2, Genesis 17:1).

9. God is holy. Therefore, lead a holy life in all areas of your life (Leviticus 19:2)

10. Live a life of integrity so that the thoughts and words and actions may align with each other and be pleasing to God. (Psalms 19:4, Matthew 3:17)

5.4 Application

I accepted the Lord Jesus as my Saviour in 1979. He had called me to His ministry in 1984. By His abundant grace, He had helped me to do my Theological and secular studies in various Colleges.

After studying till the 10th standard, I had stopped my studies due to lack of financial support from the family. My mom and my elder brother were only the bread winners since I had lost my dad at the age of four. After accepting the Lord, and when He had called me for the ministry, I began my studies again. I did my B.Th (Union Biblical Seminary-Pune); B.D (ACTC-Hyderabad); M.A (Osmania University-Hyderabad) M.Th (Religions) United Theological College-Bangalore and Ph.D (Religions at SHUATS - Prayagaraj, UP) and successfully completed the studies with the support of family and friends.

In all these years, despite the ups and downs in the life, the Lord of Living Waters gave me 'thirst' to serve Him and His people.

I am very grateful to Lord Jesus, my Saviour, "Bless the LORD, O my soul and all that is within me, bless His holy name!

Bless the LORD, O my soul, and forget not all His benefits, who forgives all my iniquity, who heals all my diseases, who redeems my life from the pit, who crowns me with steadfast love and mercy, who satisfies me with good so that your youth is renewed like the eagle's." (Psalms 103:1-5)

What is your thirst?

Eli, the priest had two sons by the names of Hopni and Phinehas. They took the priestly job because of their father. But they did not know God and they became wicked. So what were they doing?

"Eli's sons were wicked men; they had no regard for the LORD or for the priests' share of the sacrifices from the people. When any man offered a sacrifice, the priest's servant would come with a three-pronged meat fork while the meat was boiling and plunge it into the container or kettle or cauldron or cooking pot. The priest would claim for himself whatever the meat fork brought up. This is the way they treated all the Israelites who came there to Shiloh". (1 Samuel 2:12-14)

What do these three pronged forks mean? <u>These are lust for sex, thirst for money and thirst for power</u>. Now a days, many people are thirsty for these, becoming slaves and wicked by indulging in one of these three or all of these three.

But the thirst of the Lord Jesus is to take you to the rock that is higher than you, (Psalms 61:2) so that you may become a light to the nations.

As a deer panths for flowing streams, so pants my soul for you, O God. My soul 'thirsts' for God, for the living God. When shall I come and appear before God? (Psalms 42:1-2)

How much love do you have for the Lord Jesus who sacrificed himself on the cross for you? How thirsty are you to know and fulfil His plans and purposes for you? Do you have the thirst; to win perishing souls for the Lord?

Moses requested the Lord to remove his name from the Book of Life for the preservation of the people of Israel. Moses went back to God and said, "Oh, these people have committed a grave sin; they have made a god of gold for themselves. Now if You would only forgive their sin. But if not, please erase me from the book You have written." (Exodus 32:32).

So also in the New Testament, Paul said that he was ready to be cursed if necessary for the salvation of his relatives and for their blessings (Romans 9:3).

"My commandment is that you love one another as I have loved you. Greater love hath no one than this, that he lay down his life for his friends. If you do what I have commanded you, you will be my friends. A slave does not know what his master is doing, I no longer call you as slaves, but friends, because I have made known to you all the things that I have heard from my Father."

"You didn't choose me. I have appointed you and chosen you, so that you may go and bear fruit, and that your fruit may remain, that whatever you ask the Father in my name, He will grant you." This is the 'thirst' of the Lord for us. With this 'thirst', Jesus glorified the Father on earth and accomplished the task that was given to Him (John 15:16, 17:4).

If we have His 'thirst' that will enable us not only to begin the race but FINISH THE RACE for His glory and for the blessings of the Nations.

5.5 Questions to be discussed

1. What do you thirst for- money, lust or power?

2. Do you have thirst for righteousness and justice?

3. Are you quenching your teacher's thirst?

4. For the sake of perishing souls are you able to spend yourself and your resources? (2 Corinthians 12:15)

THE SIXTH WORD

6. "IT IS FINISHED". JOHN 19:30

The sour wine was offered to Jesus before his crucifixion but he refused. "And they brought Jesus to the place called Golgotha (which means Skull Place). 23 They tried to give Him wine mixed with myrrh, but He did not take it. 24 Then they crucified Him" Mark 15.22-24

But now before He gave up his spirit, Jesus had received the sour wine, He said, "It is finished," and He bowed His head and gave up His spirit (John 19:30). These words are recorded by the beloved disciple, John. This sixth word reflects the persistence and perfect love of Jesus towards the Father in heaven.

6.1 Old Testament Prophecy

Although no exact connection with this word is found in the Old Testament, many prophecies foreshadow the life, sufferings, the death and the resurrection of the Lord Jesus.

*   For instance, the Seed of woman who strikes the head of serpent points out to the Lord Jesus Christ. Genesis 3:15

*   The Passover Lamb foreshadows the sacrifice of Jesus. Exodus 12.

*   The water that gushed out from the rock when Moses strikes it, resembles Jesus Christ, the Living Waters. Numbers 20:11

*   Psalms 22.16c says, "They pierced my hands and feet", by which they hanged the Lord Jesus Christ to the Cross.

*   The Tabernacle that was built in the wilderness also resembles the Lord Jesus Christ. Hebrews 9: 1-11

*   The Priest, Melchizedek who is called the King of righteousness and the king of Salem was the prototype of the Lord Jesus Christ. Hebrews 7.

*   Isaiah 53 reflects the Suffering Servant who is none other than the Lord Jesus Christ.

The Passover lamb, the Lord Jesus was sacrificed on the cross as a ransom for many. The lamb was described very clearly in the book of Exodus chapter 12.

Tell the whole community of Israel that on the tenth day of this month they must each select an animal of the flock according to their fathers' households, one animal per household. If the household is too small for a whole animal, that person and the neighbor nearest to his house are to select one based on the combined number of people; you should apportion the animal according to what each person will eat. You must have an unblemished animal, a year-old male; you may take it from either the sheep or the goats. You are to keep it until the fourteenth day of this month; then the whole assembly of the community of Israel will slaughter the animals at twilight. It is to be eaten in one house. You may not take any of the meat outside the house, and you may not break any of its bones. Exodus 12:3-6, 46.

This was fulfilled in the Life of Jesus who takes away the sins of the World. John 1:29. This was fulfilled in the life of the Lord Jesus, the Lamb of God who took away the sin of the world. No one should be left alive on the cross after the evening. Seeing that the two robbers were still alive, they broke their legs. Because the Lord Jesus had already died, they did not break His legs but to confirm it, they stabbed Him in the side with a spear. Blood and water flowed from His side. (John 19:31)

Jesus Christ is a symbol of the sinless Passover sacrifice as it is explained in the book of Isaiah (Isaiah 53). This whole chapter explains that the Lord was satisfied with bearing our sins. Like sheep we all go astray. We have sent each of us to the path of his choice.

Jesus grew up like a tender plant. He was despised, rejected by men, a man of suffering, familiar with pain, and invisible to men. He who is despised has no appearance or beauty, He does not have the appearance that we desire. But He was wounded by our transgressions, He was crushed by our iniquities, our punishment fell upon Him, and we are healed by His wounds.

Surely He bore our sicknesses, He carried our addictions, for He laid down His life to receive death, He was chosen among the transgressors, He bore the sins of many and made intercession for those who rebelled, surely He did no injustice, there was no hypocrisy in His mouth. Yet it was the Lord's will to crush Him and cause Him to suffer, and though the Lord makes His life an offering for sin, He will see His offspring and prolong His days, and the will of the Lord will prosper in His hand. He will live long, and Jehovah's purpose will succeed through Him. He did not open his mouth when He was oppressed. He was brought as a judge for injustice, He was killed because of the wickedness of my people.

HE WAS SATISFIED WITH HIS SUFFERINGS. Seeing all these hardships of Jesus Christ, the Father was not sad but satisfied. Why is it that the Father likes to crush Him? Jesus' supreme duty is to fulfil the Father's will. Lord Jesus is satisfied that He has fulfilled the will of the Father in Heaven.

<u>Oh Dear Jesus, thousands and   thousands of tons of thanks and praises for your great sacrifice for us!</u>

Having suffered, Jesus reflected on His work and was satisfied because what He had done on the Cross was highly pleasing to the Father.

God the Father had chosen Jesus to be afflicted. He laid upon Him the iniquity of us all. It pleased Jehovah to crush Him, and He put Him to grief. The Righteous Servant bears the sins of the people and acquits many by His experience (Isaiah 53:2-12).

What was the result? It's written, "Therefore I will give Him the many as a portion and He will receive the mighty as spoil, because He submitted Himself to death.

The day will come, when God will pour out a spirit of grace and prayer on the house of David and the residents of Jerusalem, and they will look at Me whom they pierced. They will mourn for Him as one mourns for an only child and weep bitterly for Him as one weeps for a firstborn. They will come and tell about His saving deeds; they will tell a future generation what He has accomplished. (Zecha 12:10, Psalms 22:30-31)

"And I will put enmity between you and the woman, and between your offspring and hers; he will crush your head, and you will strike his heel." (Genesis 3:15)

The Lord Jesus did crush the head of the wicked Lucifer, that is the head of the serpent. Satan tried many a times to kill Jesus. But Jesus neither gave a chance nor an opportunity to Satan.

After Jesus was baptized and fasted for forty days, Satan attempted to attack Him through the three temptations (Luke 4:1- 11).

The Lord Jesus, as the Seed of a woman, came down to this world in the Name of Jesus Christ and thwarted all these efforts of Satan.

In the beginning was the Word, the Word was with God, and the Word was God. He was with God in the beginning. All things came into existence from Him, and nothing that exists was not created without Him. There was life in Him, and that life was made manifest to men. The Word became flesh and dwelt among us full of grace. May we find His glory as the glory of the only begotten Son of the Father (John 1:1-3,14).

Jesus' death on the cross fulfilled these prophecies. His last words, "It is finished," therefore refer to the completion of God's redemptive plan. Through His sacrifice, the Lord Jesus paid the penalty for sin and reconciled the human race to God. His resurrection further confirmed His victory over sin and death.

Jesus not only conquered sin and death but He also empowered His followers to do so. In order for them to do this, Jesus promised the Holy Spirit, the Third Person of the Trinity. "But you will receive power when the Holy Spirit has come on you, and you will be My witnesses in Jerusalem, in all Judea and Samaria, and to the ends of the earth" Acts 1:8 .

6.2 Fulfillment in the New Testament

The Lord Jesus spoke the sixth Word, "IT IS FINISHED" just before His death on the cross. It represents the completion of the redemptive work—the fulfillment of God's plan for human salvation— through the sacrifice of Jesus on the cross. It is atonement for the sins of all mankind. Jesus is God who takes away the sin of the world, He is portrayed as the Lamb of God. (John 1:29)

When Jesus had received the sour wine, He said, "It is finished! "Then bowing His head, He gave up His spirit (John 19:30).

"It is finished." This word is traditionally called "The Word of Triumph." Jesus' awaiting the resurrection to a new life, can be perceived to be at the end of one's earthly life.

The word *tetelestai* in Greek is used for 'it is finished'. This wording is used on business documents or receipts to indicate that a price or debt has been "paid in full". This debt is the wages of sin which is death. The debt is terrible and great. No one can pay this ransom.

The Psalmist says in Psalms 49:7-9, "Truly no man can ransom another, or give to God the price of his life, for the ransom of their life is costly and can never suffice, that he should live on forever and never see the pit. But thanks be to the Lord Jesus who paid this ransom amount neither by money nor by gold or silver but by His precious blood.

Do you not know that your bodies are temples of the Holy Spirit, who is in you, whom you have received from God? You are not your own; you were bought at a price. Therefore honor God with your bodies. (1 cor 6:19-20)

The Father in Heaven sent Jesus on a mission. His work is to redeem the mankind from their sin. This is a very difficult task. However, the Lord Jesus, the Last Adam, completed this work and said Tetelestai which means, "It is finished".

Jesus knew from the beginning what his work was and why

he came into the world.

Now His parents went to Jerusalem every year at the Feast of the Passover. When Jesus was twelve years old, they went up to Jerusalem according to the custom. And when the feast had ended, as they were returning, the boy Jesus stayed behind in Jerusalem. His parents did not realise it, but supposing Him to be in the group they went a day's journey, but then they began to search for Him among their relatives and acquaintances. When they could not find him, they returned to Jerusalem, searching for Him.

After three days they found Him in the temple, sitting among the teachers, listening to them and asking them questions. And all who heard Him were amazed at His understanding and His answers.

When His parents saw Him, they were astonished. His mother said to him, "Son, why have you treated us so? Behold, your father and I have been searching for you in great distress." He said to them, "Why were you looking for Me? Did you not know that I must be in My Father's house?"

And they did not understand the words that He spoke to them.(Luke 2:41-51).

But the question is - Who is looking for whom? Are the

parents seeking the Son, or is Jesus seeking to save all of humanity including His parents?!!!

The sixth word uttered on the cross – 'it is finished' is the end of Jesus' quest to seek and save the lost. The purpose of His coming was accomplished. By this the Father in heaven was pleased. A feast of Salvation for all mankind had been prepared and the invitation was extended to the ends of the earth.

However, a question arises for the seekers of truth. The theme of Jesus' high priestly prayer and the theme of Jesus' prayer in the Garden of Gethsemane appear to be in contrast. What is its meaning? I have fully fulfilled the task you gave me to do and glorified you on earth, Jesus had prayed as the high priest. (John 17:4)

If so, why was His prayer in the garden of Gethsemane in contrast to it? He told His disciples to stand with Him and watch with Him. Then He went across some distance and prayed that if it was so possible, my Father, let this cup pass from Me, yet not as I will, but as You will (Mat 26:39).

Who is Lord Jesus? He is divine. Both the human nature and the divine nature are present in Him. It is human nature to say "Father, if it be possible, remove this cup from me". He prayed accordingly. At the same time, with divine nature, he offered himself to do not HIS WILL but the WILL of the FATHER in HEAVEN.

Jesus knew that He was crucified for an Eternal purpose. It is the Will of God for the salvation of all the mankind. Earlier Jesus had said that He has an authority on His life, He could freely offer it and also take it back.

"For this reason the Father loves me, because I lay down My life that I may take it up again. No one takes it from Me, but I lay it down of My own accord. I have authority to lay it down, and I have authority to take it up again. This charge I have received from My Father" (John 10:17,18).

Jesus had announced the purpose of His first coming at the beginning of His earthly ministry. "He began to teach them that the Son of Man must suffer many things and be rejected by the elders, the chief priests, and the scribes; He must be killed, and then rise again after three days." He was openly talking about this (Mark 8:31-33). For even the Son of Man did not come to be served, but to serve, and to give His life — a ransom for many (Mark 10:45).

6.3 Message

A father has a job and a son also has a job assigned to Him. Lord Jesus said the same thing, "My Father has been working until now, and I am also working." (John 5:17).

"I have testimony weightier than that of John. For the works that the Father has given Me to finish—the very works that I am doing—testify that the Father has sent Me. And the Father who sent Me has Himself testified concerning Me. You have never heard His voice nor seen His form." (John 5:36-37)

From the age of twelve, Lord Jesus knew His duty or responsibility given to Him by the Father in Heaven.

In summary, this sixth word does not appear directly in the Old Testament in specific words. However, the salvation provided by the sacrifice of Jesus' life is in perfect agreement with the prophetic scriptures. It demonstrates God's transcendent and eternal love for all mankind.

This word is full of solemn truth. This 'Word' reveals that not only was Christ's earthly life completed here but also His suffering, death was completed and so the ransom payment was fully paid. Also all the prophetic scriptures about the Lord Jesus were fulfilled. The Last Adam- the Lord Jesus Christ was loyal till the end. Jesus, with loyalty, faithfulness and satisfaction, said, 'IT IS FINISHED.' (John 19:28)

God has entrusted a task to Jesus to accomplish. It was death on a cross with great humiliation and great suffering. He was born as a King, lived as a King and died as a King. He is the King of kings and the Lord of lords.

What is the prime purpose of Jesus coming to this world?

Is it for healing? Is it for feeding? Is it for delivering from the evil spirits? Is it for doing the miracles like walking on the waters and silencing the wind and waves? To raise the people from the dead?

The purpose of Jesus coming to this earth not only healing the sick but also doing the will of the Father and to offer Himself as the living sacrifice on the Cross for the redemption of the mankind.

Jesus's ministry- External:

And Jesus went throughout all the cities and villages, teaching in their synagogues and proclaiming the gospel of the kingdom and healing every disease and every affliction. When He saw the crowds, He had compassion for them, because they were harassed and helpless, like sheep without a shepherd. Then He said to His disciples, "The harvest is plentiful, but the laborers are few; therefore pray earnestly to the Lord of the harvest to send out laborers into His harvest." Matthew 9:35- 38

Jesus raised the 12 year old girl from death by speaking *'talithakumi'*. Immediately the girl rose up and began to speak. Jesus strictly charged them that no one should know this (Mark 5:43).

Jesus also healed the one who is deaf and who had difficulty in speaking by saying *'ephatha'*. He was healed instantly. Then, "He ordered them to tell no one. But the more He ordered them, the more greatly they proclaimed it. They were astonished beyond measure, saying, " He has done all things well. He makes both the deaf to hear and the mute to speak" (Mark 7:36-37).

Jesus healed many people. He cast out demons from people, made the blind see, the deaf hear, and the mute speak. He did these things to show the love of God to people, but why did He command the people. He healed not to tell anyone that He healed them? Why would He want them to keep it to themselves?

Jesus's ministry- Internal, Self Sacrifice:

Let's take a look at the heart of this humble Man. Christ Jesus came to do the will of the Father. He was intent on keeping it that way. In John 6:38, He said, "I came down from heaven, not to do my own will, but the will of Him who sent Me." He came here to do what God wants. Neither did He long for earthly praise nor human adoration. His intent was on doing what the father wanted, He had no need for human approval to do it.

His main task was the death on the cross. This is an important task because it is the Lord Jesus on the cross who has given and will give eternal life and everlasting life.

Therefore, each individual must make a decision about the Lord Jesus. What is human life! How fragile it is. Look at this body that is going to decay and die, any day or any time. But the human soul is eternal and will live forever either in heaven or in hell. Dear friends, where is your eternal destiny? With God or without Him? With God it is called 'heaven' and without God it is called 'hell'. The final decision is yours. Is it heaven or hell?

The Lord Jesus is the author and finisher of our faith (Hebrews 12:2). Though the king Solomon could not do what he preached, but he told the truth. That is, the end is better than the beginning. (Ecclesiastes 7:8)

Everyone in Christ was chosen by God before the foundation of the world. Moreover, the Word proclaims that God the Father has predestined certain works for them to do as well.

We are created in Christ Jesus to do all that God has foreordained for us to work (Ephesians 2:10).

Judas Iscariot also was chosen as one of the disciples as written in the Acts of the Apostles. He also participated in the ministry of Jesus along with other disciples.

He started the race well but missed the goal and lost his reward. So apostles prayed and appointed one person in his place (Acts 1:25).

Unlike Judas, each must do his assigned work and finish the assignment. Finishing well is more important than beginning.

The aforesaid sufferings, curses and dark day of the Lord Jesus on the cross became a blessing and the brightest day for all mankind.

According to the Gospel of John, the word "finished" is a greatest accomplishment. John the disciple presents his gospel in a different and 'royal' way. Unlike other gospels, Jesus did not tremble while carrying the cross. He was neither presented to nor any trial had taken place before the highest Jewish council, called the Sanhedrin. Jesus was directly taken to the governor and the Roman judge Pilate. He introduced Jesus to the Jewish people by saying, "Here is your King" (John

19:14).

As written in the rest of the gospels, the Lord Jesus went on his journey to the cross, never faltering or falling. Even so, the way of the cross is majestic and is presented as full of dignity for "Jesus was on His own and He went forth bearing His cross" (John 19:17).

Another important point is that in the Gospel of John, at the top of the cross, it is clearly written INRI. It is Latin." Jesus Nazarenes, Rex Yudeorum". "Jesus of Nazareth, King of the Jews" (John 19:19).

It is not written that the death of the Lord Jesus is unexpected. He did not die by a cardiac arrest. But He voluntarily "submitted" his soul. This means that till the last minute of His breath, Jesus was in full control. Jesus simply surrendered his soul to the Father in heaven. Here lies another mysterious truth. That is, His death paved the way for the promised coming of the Holy Spirit.

Holy Spirit

The crucifixion and death of the Lord Jesus was not the end of His life, but the beginning of the age of the Holy Spirit, the third person of the Trinity. The Gospel of John reveals much more about the revelation of the Holy Spirit, than the other gospel writers.

The Lord Jesus spoke of living waters in John 4:10. Likewise during the feast of tabernacles (John 7:37- 39). He refers to these living waters as the Holy Spirit. And I will ask the Father, and he will give you another Helper, to be with you forever, even the Spirit of truth, whom the world cannot receive, because it neither sees him nor knows him. You know him, for he dwells with you and will be in you (John 14:16- 17).

The word Paraclete means advocate, counsellor, helper or comforter or benefactor. "These things I have spoken to you while I am still with you. But the Helper, the Holy Spirit, whom the Father will send in My name, He will teach you all things and bring to your remembrance all that I have said to you" (John 14:26).

6.4 Application

The Bible says that the end is better than the beginning. The Lord Jesus has finished His race well. He overcame many temptations and trials. One of the most important requirements to finish well is, one need to empty him/herself. Only then will we be filled with the Holy Spirit.

As the Bible proclaims that whoever invites Jesus Christ

into their hearts will become the temple of God (Revelation 3.20, 1 Corinthians 3.16). King Solomon completed the world famous temple in seven years. But do you know how much time God is taking to build this 'living temple' that God is building? God Himself is the architect and the builder of this temple (Hebrews 11.10). We are the rock and He is a great sculptor. He is carving a sculpture. How beautiful it is. Are you observing how the construction of the living temple is going on, are you cooperating or providing any materials!!!

There are three things that we need to have in us in order to provide these materials -

FAT - (Faithful; Accountable; Teachable)

Faithful: Having 'faith' in God is different than leading a 'faithful' life.

My eyes favor the faithful of the land so that they may sit down with me. The one who follows the way of integrity may serve me (Psalms 101.6).

Accountable: Every believer needs to give an account of himself / herself - about the thoughts, about the words and about the actions of their life. Each of us will give an account of himself to God (Romans 14.12).

Teachable: Teach-ability comes by listening and be willing to learn. Bible says, "Its good to have many counselors. Good advise must be received whether it comes from young or old; from rich or poor".

Moses the chosen man of God was leading the God's army, the people of Israel, were 603,550 (Num 1.46). This number will be more, if both women and children were added. For this group, Moses was not only a prophet but also a judge. From morning till evening he was sitting with all the children of Israel who came to him seeking for justice and help.

Once it so happened that the Midian priest, Jethro, the father in law of Moses came to visit him, while he was in his office. He observed that all the day, Moses was attending to the needs of the Israelites as they would stand before him for justice. Having observed the situation, Jethro, the Midianite priest told his son in law, 'what you are doing is not right'.

Moses did not say, 'uncle please mind your own business', rather he listened to him. As the result, today we see village courts, tahasil court, district court, high court and finally the Supreme Court to help the people without much trouble.

Moses has a teachable spirit and was willing to learn.

By following this 'FAT' principle, I want to make it my aim that the meditations of my heart and the words of my mouth and even the works of my hand be acceptable to God, my rock and my Saviour. Psalms 19.14

So that I may hear His approval, "This is my dear son, in whom I am well pleased'. By this we also like Jesus can say joyfully, "It is finished".

6.5 Questions to be discussed

1. Are you faithfully doing the work that is assigned to you, big or small? Are you finishing well?

2. Do you own your thoughts / words / actions? Are you ready to stand before the throne of his Judgement ?

3. Do you have the mind to learn? Are you teachable?

4. What precautions would you take to 'finish well'?

THE SEVENTH WORD

7. "FATHER, INTO YOUR HANDS I COMMIT MY SPIRIT". LUKE 23:46.

Luke writes[1] that the sun has disappeared and the curtain was torn down from the top to the bottom (Luke 23.45). Then Jesus spoke this last word.

"Father, into your hands I commit my spirit" (Luke 23:46). This is the seventh word spoken by the LORD Jesus on the cross. This seventh word is called "re -union". The LORD Jesus gave Himself in complete loving trust to God the Father in heaven.

7.1 Old Testament Prophecy

"Into thy hand I commit my soul. Jehovah, faithful God, thou hast redeemed me. (Psalms 31:5) These words are spoken by David.

This is not a prayer request, but refers to speaking to the

---

[1] The gospel writers Matthew and Mark wrote the 7th word was spoken by Jesus soon after the 4th word, Eli Eli lama sabakthani… and the curtain was torn down from the top to bottom, after Jesus gave up His spirit (Mat 27.47-50, mark 15.38).

Father in complete trust and surrendering himself. In this psalm David is in fear of the enemy from all directions. However, he expresses unshakable faith in God. He strongly believes that those who know and love God, for them all things work together for good. Because they have been called by God according to His glorious purpose (Romans 8:28). So David invites everyone to love him to receive the favour of God.

Further King David reflects his relationship with God in this Psalms 31

I hate those who pay regard to worthless idols, but I trust in the LORD. I will rejoice and be glad in Your steadfast love, because You have seen my affliction; You have known the distress of my soul, and You have not delivered me into the hand of the enemy; You have set my feet in a broad place.

Because of all my adversaries I have become a reproach, especially to my neighbours, and an object of dread to my acquaintances; those who see me in the street flee from me. I have been forgotten like one who is dead; I have become like a broken vessel. For I hear the whispering of many—terror on every side!— as they scheme together against me, as they plot to take my life.

But I trust in You, O LORD; I say, "You are my God."

My times are in your hand; rescue me from the hand of my enemies and from my persecutors! Make Your face shine on Your servant; save me in Your steadfast love!

Oh, how abundant is Your goodness, which You have stored up for those who fear You and worked for those who take refuge in You, in the sight of the children of mankind! Love the LORD, all you His saints! The LORD preserves the faithful but abundantly repays the one who acts in pride. Be strong, and let your heart take courage, all you who wait for the LORD! (Psalms 31: 6 - 8,11- 16, 19, 23)

This crucifixion incident was not shocking news for Jesus. The cross was, just like one of the daily events of Jesus' life and ministry. As He used to enter the temple every day, as He used to go to the place of worship. As He preaches daily according to His custom, as He goes to the prayer hall according to custom, in the same way He entered death on the Cross.

The death of the Lord Jesus on the Cross is neither surprising nor unexpected to him. He willingly offered His life as a Perfect Sacrifice, once for all. He committed Himself into the hands of God the Father. Through this event, the Father and the Son are reunited. They are going to be united for Eternity (Luke 4.16, 21.37, 22.39, Mark 10.1).

7.2 Fulfilment in the New Testament

The last words spoken by the Lord Jesus are recorded in Luke 23:46.

He cried out with a loud voice, "Father, into your hands I commit my spirit," and surrendered himself. He breathed his last physical breath. This word and deed of Jesus was a complete trust in God. And having completed the faithful work, He gave himself to the Father with joy and happiness (John 10:15).

Father - Son relationship:

God is Trinity. God the Father, God the Son, God the Holy Spirit. In the beginning was the Word, the Word was with God, the Word was God (John 1:1).

The Father consecrated the Lord Jesus and sent Him into the world. Jesus said, 'Believe Me that I am in the Father, and the Father is in Me, or because of the works. But I do as the Father commanded Me, so that the world may know that I love the Father (John 10:36, 14:11, 31).

Jesus said, "I and the Father are one." I came from the Father into this world. And He said to them that He is leaving the world and going to the Father. Jesus Christ knew the Father and honoured Him. He loved the Lord the Father, and always did as the Father commanded. Jesus loved the Father and obeyed His commandments. Jesus knows the Father and the Father also knows the Son. Jesus said that He is the good shepherd and He will lay down His life for the sheep. (John 10:30, 16:28, 10:15, 8:49, 14:31, 15:10)

Have you noticed, how deep and loving the relationship between Father and Son is.

According to John 12:49, the Father who has sent Jesus Christ to this world, has commanded Him what to say and what to speak.

What is the difference between 'saying' and 'speaking'?

Saying is in response to others words/actions. Speaking is to speak on one's own initiative.

There are three commandments in it...what I shall say... what I shall speak...what I shall do.

1. What shall I say means ... to reply others of their words or actions

Ex: All the religious leaders and the criminals on both sides of Jesus were insulting Him. In this situation, what to say?

What should be His response? Jesus blessed them and said to the Father, 'forgive them for they do not know what they are either speaking or doing'.

Secondly, what to speak, the Father also gave the order that He Himself should speak about according to the situation. That is why, Solomon the wise, said that a well-spoken word is like golden fruit set on silver platters. (Proverbs 25:11).

About 3,40,823 (three lakh forty thousand and eight hundred and twenty three) people came from all the tribes of Judah to make David king according to God's wonderful plan. These belong to the tribe of Issacharites (1 Chronicles 12:32). Out of this number there are about 200 people who had understanding of the times, to know what Israel ought to do. How blessed are we, if we have this type of people with us today. This word is like a golden fruit on a silver platter.

In John 12:49, what should be the commandments received from the Father? Jesus knows all the times – what to say; what to speak and what to do.

What commandments do we need today from the Father?

We need from the Father in Heaven-

1.   What to think, what not,

2.   What to see, what not,

3.   What to speak, what not,

4.   What to listen, what not

5.   What to do, what not.

The above 2, 3 &4 points look like what we see in three pictures of monkeys: Do not see evil; do not speak evil and do not listen to evil. Along with it, the most important is that one should not think and act evil.

All the above five points admonish the body of Christ to control five senses. As the horse is controlled by one 'bridle'; a disciple of Christ needs at least five 'bridles' to control his/her God given Temple, the body. So to fulfil Father's commandments one need to make a good dedication, determination and discipline to follow the same, like one of the Old Testament Scribes. Now Ezra had determined in his heart to study the law of the LORD, obey it, and teach its statutes and ordinances in Israel (Ezra 7:10).

Everything is commanded by God the Father. The thoughts, words and actions of Father and the Son are not separate. Both are in the same page. That is why Lord Jesus said many times. I am in the Father and the Father is in Me (John 12:49, 17:22).

Jesus Christ is the beloved Son of the Father. So the Father thinks through, speaks through and works through His Son, so also now through the Body of Christ, the Church, you and me.

7.3 Message

The Last Scenario of the Universe:

We are blessed people. Because our faith in Christ is not for this life time alone rather its for eternity. If our faith is only for this life time, then we are the most miserable people on this planet.

God has revealed a lot of things to St. Paul, about the Last Adam, that is about Lord Jesus Christ and His Church.

Jesus, the Lord conquered the death and rose again. He is also coming again to draw His church closer to Him.

Bible says that everyone who believes in Him will have resurrection in his own order.

For as in Adam all die, so also in Christ all will be made alive. But each in his own order: Christ, the first fruits; afterward, at His coming, those who belong to Christ. Then comes the end, when He hands over the kingdom to God the Father, when He abolishes all rule and all authority and power. For He must reign until He puts all His enemies under His feet. The last enemy to be abolished is death. For God has put everything under His feet. But when it says "everything" is put under Him, it is obvious that He who puts everything under Him is the exception. And when everything is subject to Christ, then the Son Himself will also be subject to the One who subjected everything to Him, so that God may be all in all (1 Corinthians 15:22-28).

Do you know what is the 'beginning and the end of the creation?' Bible says its 'God' alone knows it. For this reason, God's Name is 'Alpha and Omega' the Beginning and the End.

Genesis 1:1 says, 'In the beginning, God created the heavens and the earth'. John the disciple writes, In the beginning was the Word, and the Word was with God, and the Word was God. He was with God in the beginning. All things were created through Him, and apart from Him not one thing was created that has been created. John 1:1-3

What is the last verse of the Bible? We may say it is in

Revelation 22:21. But the last scene of this universe is recorded in 1 Corinthians 15:28.

"And when everything is subject to Christ, then the Son Himself will also be subject to the One who subjected everything to Him, so that God may be all in all."

By this verse, we know that Jesus entrusted two things to God the Father. The first is the Kingdom, and the second is, Himself.

God is One, the Trinity. That is, God the Father and God the Son, God the Holy Spirit. Trinitarian God is One in Thought, Word, Deed and especially in Nature. It is a great mystery. May God Himself reveal Himself to all of us by His grace either before He comes the second time to this planet or before the end of our life.

"I came from the Father and entered into the world, but in turn, I am leaving the world and going back to the Father" (John 16:28). For just as the Father has life in Himself, thus He has granted the Son to have life in Himself. John 5:26

No one takes it from Me, but I lay it down on My own. I have the right to lay it down, and I have the right to take it up again. I have received this command from My Father."(John 10:18).

This verse makes it very clear that no one killed the Lord Jesus but He offered Himself willingly. He sacrificed his life for the whole world. He offered Himself as our only Saviour to save us from eternal hell.

It's the natural phenomena to notice that the sun rises in the east. So also it's very natural to say that there is no atonement without shedding of the blood. (Hebrews 9:22)

The Life giving sacrifice of Jesus should be a model for every Christian to follow. Whether it is illness, or financial deficiencies, or even any dire circumstances, one need to take refuge in God alone.

Everything should be submitted to God the Father like Jesus. So also St. Paul surrendered himself and his resources gladly for the sake of the Kingdom of God and for His church. 2 Corinthians 12:15.

In Romans 8:31-33. St Paul is asking, What then are we to say about these things? If God is for us, who is against us? He did not even spare His own Son but offered Him up for us all; how will He not also with Him grant us everything? Who can bring an accusation against God's elect?

So also St. Peter says, Humble yourselves, therefore, under the mighty hand of God, so that He may exalt you at the proper time, casting all your care on Him, because He cares about you. Be serious! Be alert! Your adversary the Devil is prowling around like a roaring lion, looking for anyone he can devour. Resist him and be firm in the faith, knowing that the same sufferings are being experienced by your fellow believers throughout the world (1 Peter 5:6-9).

See the promise of God —"I will not leave you, I will not forsake you." Even if you are surrounded by the bonds of death, God will release you. And make you to be fruitful. He is omnipotent. omniscient omnipresent Nothing is impossible for Him.

You may think "I have lost everything in my life, no hope left. It is a mess. There is no one to help. You may be thinking 'death' is only the answer. FEAR NOT. The Lord Jesus came for you alone. He is the One who will be with you. This Immanuel God will empower you to overcome your situation.

God is the giver of divine peace. He gives abundant life now and eternal life in future. It is God who desires to fill you so that you may overflow in your life and ministry.

"Jesus the Lord," there are two words in it. Jesus means Saviour. The Lord means King, Ruler, Master. In most cases, people accept God as the Saviour only but not as the Lord, or Master. Those who accept God as saviour, they are only called the 'believers'. But who accept God as their Master and King, they are called 'disciples'. Jesus commissioned the disciples to go and make 'disciples' of all the nations. God needs, our nation needs and the church needs 'disciples'. Are you a believer or a disciple?

7.4 Application

Lord Jesus, who willingly gave His life on the cross, uttered these words in a solemn and contented voice, "Father, into Your hands I entrust My spirit." Saying this, He breathed His last.

The last words of the Lord Jesus clearly reveal His faith and absolute trust in God the Father, even as He suffered and wandered through the valley of terrible death. Thus Jesus gave the gift of eternal life to all who believe in him. In the Christian life and ministry, THE END IS MORE

IMPORTANT THAN THE BEGINNING.

I came to know Jesus Christ as my personal Saviour and the Lord in June 1979. God spoke to me through the Word of God from 2 Samuel 18:33. David was lamenting for his son Abshalom.

And the king was deeply moved and went up to the chamber over the gate and wept. And as he went, he said, "O my son Absalom, my son, my son Absalom! Would I had died instead of you, O Absalom, my son, my son!"

When I came across this passage, I realized that it is the love of the Lord Jesus Christ who died for me on the cross of Calvary. He was buried and rose again on the third day. He is the Living God.

Through the prophet Isaiah, the Lord by His abundant grace, called me for the ministry in 1984. And I heard the voice of the Lord saying, "Whom shall I send, and who will go for us?" Then I said, "Here I am! Send me." And he said, "Go, and say to this people: (Isaiah 6:8-9)

Though I was serving the Lord since 22 years. I realized that 'life' is more important than 'ministry'. We can see this truth in the very beginning of Jesus' life. God the Father testified of Him, at the time of His baptism, before His ministry had begun.

Jesus came to the shore from the water. Behold, the heavens were opened, and I saw the Spirit of God descending like a dove and coming upon Him. And a voice came from heaven saying, Behold, this is my beloved Son, in whom I am well pleased. Matthew 3:16-17

God also revealed this in the Old Testament by sending Samuel the prophet to Bethlehem. "I will send you to Jesse the Bethlehemite, for I have provided for myself a king among his sons."··· and I will show you what you shall do. And you shall anoint for me him whom I declare to you." Samuel went as the Lord commanded him and invited Jesse'sons.

When they came, he looked on Eliab and thought, "Surely the LORD's anointed is before him. "But the LORD said to Samuel, "Do not look on his appearance or on the height of his stature, because I have rejected him. For the LORD sees not as man sees: man looks on the outward appearance, but the LORD looks on the heart." 1 Samuel 16:3-7

Since then, I have realized that 'internal life' is more important than 'external ministry'. BEING IS MORE IMPORTANT THAN DOING. I am trying to practice the same from 2006- to walk with God in sincerity. This is the first and far most thing in the life. The second thing is to serve God faithfully even in small things.

Currently I am committed to both internal and external purity. I am challenging myself daily, to say, "Follow me as I am following Christ." (1 Corinthians 11:1)

For this reason, I am re-committing my life to the Lord Jesus who sacrificed His life for me. May the Lord Jesus help all of us to live like Him, to declare and demonstrate the Good News; among the Nations.

Jesus said, "Father, into your hands I commend my spirit" (Luke 23:46).

7.5 Questions to be discussed

1. Do you know the true God who created the universe?

2. Have you received the eternal kingdom prepared for you?

3. Explain your trust and commitment to the Lord in all situations?

4. Are you surrendering yourself to the Father's will in all situations?

Conclusion

J esus' words on the cross were not merely seven words. These are precious packs of diamonds that bring value to the mankind. These are the Words that lead humanity from darkness to light. These are the Words that lead from curse to blessing. These are the Words that lead from slavery to freedom. These are the Words of Jesus Christ that lead from death to Eternal Life.

These seven Words are rather seven messages are transformative causes for the people on this planet. God who gives abundant life in this world and eternal life in the world to come.

At the end, let's recap the Words of the Lord Jesus who was born as king; lived as king; died as king; rose again from death as king and reigns as king!

1. "Father, forgive them, for they know not what they do" Know who your God is, know who you are. Confess your sins and ask for forgiveness and receive it.

2. "Today you are with me in paradise" Make good use of time. Live today, as if this is the last moment of the day. Receive forgiveness and forgive others.

3.	"Mother, this is your son" and to the disciple, "this is your mother". Any information should be given to both. The communication should be transparent. First, in your personal life, make sure that your thoughts, your words and your works are pleasing to God. Then in family life, husband and wife should come together and build their family with both parents. Make your home as mini-heaven. Finally, you should have a good reputation in the social life. God should be pleased by your personal life, family life, ministry life and social life.

4.	"My God, My God, why have you forsaken me". The Lord Jesus, the Creator of the Universe, the Saviour of the World who loves you most will never forsake you though everyone may leave. His Name is Immanuel so He will be with you. So take courage. Cling on to Him, be patient and wait. Don't look back, the Christian life is always going forward.

5.	"I thirst" As a deer longs for running water, you should have hunger for righteousness. The running water is always fresh. This longing for fresh waters/ fresh food-Manna, must increase day by day. Abide in the Word of God and seek His presence always. That will bring good thoughts, good words, good fellowship, good deeds, and good testimony. In Psalms 1, a tree planted by streams of water yields its fruit in its season and its leaf does not wither. That is, the testimony should not be corrupted. Every Christian should lead a model life in person, in the family, in the church and in community. If the leaf remains green, the fruit will come in its due time.

6. "Finished" Jesus Christ, the last Adam had accomplished His mission, so He said 'tetelestai' which means, 'It is finished'. One of the greatest and precious things in the world is, not the beginning of a work but the completion of it. Finishing well is very important. Christian life is not a sprint but it is marathon. Need to run steadily till the end. The race needs to be completed. St Paul says, I have fought the good fight, I have finished the race, I have kept the faith (2 Timothy 4:7). A Christian not only needs to keep faith till the end but living faithfully even in small things is very important. Only way we can all say like St Paul and like our Lord and Saviour Jesus Christ is, 'It is finished'.

7. "Father, into your hands I commit my spirit" We should surrender our life and offer everything to God because everything belongs to Him. All earth belongs to God. Sun, moon and stars belong to God. All believers and disciples

belong to God since He has purchased them with the precious blood of the Lord Jesus Christ (Colossians 1:15-16,Psalms 24:1, 1 Corinthians 6:19-20)

There is no one else than the Lord Jesus who is the source and shelter of our well-being. He is the Chief Shepherd. That is why we should always commit and surrender ourselves as the Lord Jesus did.

Asatoma Sadgamya- Lead from untruth to truth   Jesus said, I am the Truth

Tamasoma Jyotirgamaya - Lead from darkness to light. Jesus said, I am the light of the world

Mrityorma Amritangamaya - Lead from death to eternal life – Jesus said, I am the Life and I am the Resurrection.

In order to bless the mankind lavishly, God came down to this world in the name of Jesus Christ. As He proclaimed the purpose of His coming to this planet, Jesus was crucified for us. He died and was buried. On the third day, as He said in the beginning, He rose from the death and appeared to many for around forty days. He proved that He was alive and that He has great plan for each and everyone on this planet. So He said, as the Father has sent Me, so also I am sending you. Go and make disciples of all the nations. Lo I am with you till the end of the

Age. There will be a final judgment for every person. Each one gets rewards according to their thoughts, words and deeds.

Even now, there is a golden opportunity. If anyone does not know Him, they may know and accept Him by seeking His forgiveness. Please open your heart and receive Him as the Saviour and the Lord of your life. He will give you abundant life now and the eternal life in future for His glory and for the blessings to the Nations. To God be the glory forever and ever. Amen.

Footnotes

[1] Rajeswari, Rajan Sunder: "Real and imagined women'. London Routledge, 1993.

[2] www//https:thoughtco.com (19th April,2024); also see, Hawley, John Stratton. 'Sat: The blessings and Curse" New York: Oxford University Press, 1994.

[3] Upetri,p 46

[4] Opcit, Hawley, p163

DISCLAIMER

This book, **"The Seven Words from the Cross,"** explores the final words of Jesus Christ as recorded in the Bible. The interpretations and reflections presented here are based on the author's personal understanding and research. They are meant to inspire and encourage readers in their spiritual journey.

Please note that this book is not intended to serve as a definitive theological or doctrinal statement. Readers are encouraged to seek additional perspectives and study the scriptures further. Any errors or omissions are unintentional and are the sole responsibility of the author.

Thank you for reading and may you find peace and enlightenment through these words.

May I Ask You for a Small Favor?

First, I want to thank you for reading this book. You could have chosen any other book, but you took mine, and I appreciate this.

I hope you got a few actionable insights that can impact your daily life positively.

Can I ask for 30 seconds more of your time?

I'd love it if you could leave a review of the book. That will help me grow my readership by encouraging folks to take a chance on my books.

Keeping it straight - reviews are the lifeblood of any author.

It will take less than a minute of your time, but it will help me reach more people.

Please provide the review at the store where you bought this book. I'd love to see it. Thanks for your support.